140 GOATS & A GUITAR

THE STORIES BEHIND SOME KIND OF CURE

DAVID BERKELEY

140 GOATS & A GUITAR

THE STORIES BEHIND
SOME KIND OF CURE

ALBUMS BY DAVID BERKELEY

Some Kind of Cure

Strange Light

Live from Fez

After the Wrecking Ships

The Confluence

For more information about David Berkeley's music and tour dates, please visit www.davidberkeley.com.

The road to Tralonca.

CONTENTS

To download *Some Kind of Cure*
go to davidberkeley.com/store
and enter: sp2xrqj53d5u

This book consists of thirteen essays that describe what inspired each of the thirteen songs on my album Some Kind of Cure. *The suggestion is that you move through the book alternating between text and music, reading a piece and then listening to its corresponding song. After each story, you will find the lyrics to the song it sets up.*

Because no one likes to see a phrase like "batteries not included," enclosed is a personal download code for you to access the songs on the album for free.

Thank you for reading and listening. In this bright and noisy world, where there are so many forces competing for your time and attention, I'm grateful that you have chosen to spend a little time with my words and music.

Although I have changed many of the names in the essays and a few details to protect people's privacy, the anecdotes are as true as my memory allows.

I remain,
David Berkeley

INTRODUCTION

The directions were barely legible. They were written in French. A man had scribbled them on the back of a business card. The name and address on the front of the card were of a used car dealer on the outskirts of Nice. It was December, already getting dark, and the dealership was about to close. So we raced around one confusing traffic circle after another, trying desperately to make out the street signs.

We had spent the morning on the famous stone beach beside the Mediterranean, listening to the click and hiss of the waves on the rocks. For the rest of the day, we navigated the aisles of the massive Carrefour—France's equivalent to Walmart—under fluorescent lights, buying all the baby things we would need for our year abroad: a travel crib, a stroller, a high chair, boxes of diapers and a car seat. Our rental car was due back later that night, and we were slated to board a ferry early the next morning for Corsica.

We were going for my wife's fieldwork. Sarah was getting a PhD in cultural anthropology and was doing research on the Corsican effort to reclaim and revitalize their traditional ways of life. We would be living in a tiny mountain village in the interior of the island. Sarah was not studying under any professor, was not affiliated with any ongoing research. We had a lady's name and number written on the first page of a blank book. She had agreed by email to rent us her flat. Other than this woman, we had no contacts. We knew no one, and no one knew us.

After two days of failed attempts finding a suitable car, we had this one last lead. But as the five o'clock bells began to ring, it looked like we weren't going to make it. I wasn't sure what we would do then. Delay our departure? Or maybe carry all our things on board the boat and try to buy a car on Corsica?

Ready to throw in the towel, I spotted the sign. Though the guy was already locking up, he took pity on us and showed us a couple cars. There, in a sense, our journey began: in a dimly lit office full of cigarette smoke, a flickering TV playing some French gossip show, Sarah toddling around with our one-year-old son Jackson, and me—sitting at the desk of an unshaven used car dealer who was itching to go home—trying to negotiate a deal with the maybe twenty French words I knew.

As a songwriter, you could say that my whole life is built around being able to express myself. But with the light dwindling outside, the jet lag kicking in and an increasingly grumpy child, I found myself unable to understand anything he was asking me, anything that was going on. I had no idea how to say what I needed to say. We were moving to Corsica for a year, and this would be just the first of many awkward negotiations and uncomfortable moments. Although my language skills got better and better, interactions like this were only amusing in retrospect.

With Sarah's help, shouting translations over her shoulder, I managed somehow to broker the deal. And though slightly unsure what we had just bought or what we had signed away, we drove off with huge relief in a little Renault Twingo into the Mediterranean night. It was shaped vaguely like a mini van, but maybe a quarter of the size, with only two doors and a hatchback (a "three-door," they call it). We cruised back to our hotel along the Riviera with the windows rolled down and big smiles on our faces. For the first time since the prospect of moving to Corsica had arisen, we felt only excitement about the adventure set to begin.

Then morning came. With better light, we made three unfortunate realizations: 1) The car was actually a surprisingly bright shade of turquoise. 2) It had no air conditioning. 3) There was virtually no chance it was going to fit all of our crap.

I spent much of the early hours trying every possible packing configuration and was just about to give up when I discovered the extra space in the spare tire well.

I crammed everything I could into that compartment, even stuffing socks into the space inside the spare itself. Then, inspired by this small success, I threw away the car's manuals and filled the glove compartment, the center console and the spaces in the doors. I still wasn't sure all three doors would close until I got Jackson and Sarah into their seats, until I wedged myself in. But miraculously the doors shut. We fit. And so long as we didn't have to open the windows, it looked like we might just make it.

I turned the key, and Leela (as Jackson came to call her) started smoothly. We held our collective breath, wondering if she'd have the power to get all of our weight up the ramp of the parking garage. To all our amazement, she did. She didn't move fast, but she did move. So with the back of the car nearly scraping the ground, with our stuff literally pressing in on us from all sides, with zero mobility and virtually no visibility, we rolled alongside the coast toward Toulon, where we caught our big boat to Corsica.

***

Our senses awoke immediately when the ferry reached the old and weathered port of Bastia. The air was incredibly clean and clear. The light magnificent. The smells, though, were the most intoxicating—a medley of mint and celery root, of cinnamon and syrup that wafted from the hills and would drift into our bedroom once we found our village and moved in. It was silent there. It still is. Corsica is a magical place and our time there was too. But the magic, like all magic, was not just positive. Our year was also scary, at times uncomfortable, never totally comprehensible.

Corsica is powerfully beautiful. Culturally, though, it is often quite closed and inhospitable. Our village didn't get many visitors. And Corsicans are notoriously hostile toward tourists. There was a popular child's t-shirt that read "Bienvenue à la Corse…Bon Chance," (Welcome to Corsica…Good Luck). Our little over-stuffed car (and my efforts to pack it) was a good metaphor for our feelings about our adventure. We tried to pack everything into that car and into our heads that we might need. In the end, little of that helped. The challenges were more fundamental. Solutions would take time, and some never came.

***

Life moved slowly in our village. A bread truck rolled up into the square every morning at some point between eight and nine, honking a nasal *wa wa waah waah wa wa waaaaaah* to let everyone know it had arrived. I would buy a baguette from the old lady who would climb behind the driver's seat and sell her loaves out of the little truck's back door. When Jackson was with me, she would say "comme, il est beau," give him a free pan au chocolat, and tell me with a wink that my wife and I should hurry and have another child. A vegetable man came by on Tuesdays. The fish truck drove through on Wednesdays around lunchtime. Saturday afternoon, after the sieste, the butcher parked in the square for an hour or so. Those trucks and the bells that rang atop our village church demarcated our time there, time that for me was spent with Sarah on one excursion after another, or hiking with Jackson through the wild mountains, or writing songs.

The rhythm of life was addictive. Meals were slow. Nothing was rushed. When the day was done, it was done. You said hello to everyone. There was always time for that. Greeting rituals were a huge deal. Depending on your relationship, you either shook hands or gave the "bisous" (kiss on both cheeks). You never merely waved. This took a lot of getting used to and was at times the hardest thing to get the hang of. When we got to bisous status with certain people it was a huge accomplishment. If someone snubbed us, it was devastating. At times these greeting rituals were tedious. In the end, they pulled our world into relief and reminded us that friends and family were worth slowing down for.

We were on Corsica through all the seasons. The changes would come subtly and then be total. These changes would alter the music I was working on, either literally influencing lyrical choices or just by altering my mood. The hillside below our village turned green. Then white flowers spread. Eventually yellow followed and then purple. Then blackberries were everywhere. Then the brush and leaves went orange. Then all was red. We came in the winter, and the winter was back again when we left. We shared in birthdays and celebrations. We were invited to family picnics and gatherings. We were there when people died.

I tend to write a lot of songs when I am in flux. Moving was nothing new to us. But this was the most extreme move we had done. There were almost as many people living in the apartments on our floor in the building we left in Brooklyn as lived in our entire village. It didn't seem that anyone on the island spoke English. And it was our first move with a young child. It is the internal unrest that inspires me most, and as picturesque as Corsica was, this move definitely brought some internal unrest. Songwriting is how I deal with and articulate those feelings. So I wrote a lot of songs.

I would take a notebook and my guitar and find a spot, on a stone wall, on a tree stump, on a rock beside a stream. This is what I do wherever I am, be it a park bench in Brooklyn or a back porch in Atlanta. I try to bring something forth. There is always a mystery to the process. If it weren't that way, if songwriting was always formulaic and I could control it, I don't think it would captivate me. It is a living thing fraught with both anxiety and wonder.

Most songs begin as lines jotted into a book I carry. Sometimes I write pages of thoughts and descriptions before I pick up my guitar and have any sense of a melody or a form. Most of my songs begin without intention.

Often they start from something quite small, a strange or uncomfortable story or situation, perhaps just a mood or a hope—a wish for escape, a need for comfort, an overwhelming surge of love for my family, a burning desire to make things in their lives okay.

Melodies appear out of nowhere. Sometimes they come intact. Sometimes I stumble into them as I find notes on my guitar. There is an inherent music in some words and phrases, and when I'm lucky, I can hear that music. Sometimes emotions are strong enough that words come out with melody, almost like a chant or a wail. I write about the emotions I feel, the images I see. Over time I discover some rhythm and rhyme scheme in what I'm writing and, helped by the structure, the phrases turn into longer lines. Fragments of melodies stretch into whole forms.

***

Corsica was an amazing place to work. Corsican culture is a culture of singers. The island gave me a new palette, new colors, new images. When I look back on it now, our whole time on that island seems almost heavenly. The way our village hung on the mountainside, the morning fog we would watch creeping closer until it wrapped around us like a robe, the cadence of the language. I miss it all. When I think about little routines from our year, like hanging our laundry on our clothesline, closing and opening the shutters, filling our glass jug with water from the spring, dumping spent ash from our fire out over the hillside, everything has a romance about it. I was often acutely aware of my place in space and time and how I would likely never be there again. The images I saw worked themselves into the music I wrote. The ashes, the shutters, the bells, the chestnut trees, the wind, the old men, the death. I sucked in the scents and sounds of the island with a hunger that I hadn't had since I was a child.

Other times, my life on Corsica was like anywhere else—a place where I lived and went through my day, my job, my chores. My mood on those days was determined by more mundane things, things that would have determined my mood even if we were still in New York. If I was in the middle of a song that excited me, if Jackson and Sarah were okay, then I was happy and alive. But if I was struggling through a song, if Jackson wasn't feeling well, if Sarah was worried, if no one could understand the things I was trying to say, then I was lonely, my stomach would knot, and I would long to be out of that village and off that island.

It was often those moments, the hard ones, that led to songs, for those were the times I picked up my guitar. There were many moments where I found myself wondering how and why I ended up where I was. One day I'm trying to understand what a Corsican doctor is telling me about how to medicate my son's ear infection and then hoping that the pharmacist gave me the right drug. The next day a guy hands me a rifle and asks me to shoot at a fox should it cross my path. One day I make a fool of myself trying to help my neighbors chop wood. The next day I'm ridiculed at the butcher for ordering a cut of meat normally fed to animals. One night I find myself forcing fried fish heads (eyes and all) into my mouth after being told they were specially prepared for us. The next day I'm trying to guard Jackson against a herd of aggressive goats. All these moments were disorienting and left me feeling out of control, only half a person. If they were funny, great. But if they weren't, and most weren't until much later, they left me reeling, in a sense, unable to stand up for myself or my family, wondering what I was doing and when I would feel like myself again.

Still when we left the island, I found myself missing it powerfully, like I had woken from a long and mysterious dream and wanted to get back to sleep so I could explore it more. Soon after I returned to America, I started recording a new album consisting largely of the songs I wrote while there. I needed the process of diving into the music to both continue living in our village and to cope with the often-overwhelming cultural shift that returning to America brought. We moved to Atlanta, and suburban life assaulted us. It couldn't have been more different from our stone home in the mountains. I was thrust suddenly back into lanes of slow-moving traffic, the aisles of Target, into a sort of sleepwalking existence where I knew the language and routine so well that I didn't have to think before I spoke or acted.

We welcomed the ease when we got back, for sure. I talked quickly and incessantly to anyone and everyone I could. Particularly in regards to our then two-year-old Jackson, it was so nice not to have to work so hard to find playgrounds or friends, daycare or food, to understand the doctor. But I also felt myself losing that hard magic that was Corsica. Recording helped. Songs are always my best stamp on a time and a place. Pictures and videos may bring you back, but they do it in a jarring, isolated way. Suddenly there's an image in your hand or on your screen. Then it's gone. Pictures are framed. Songs are different. They occupy no space. They blend into and fill our worlds. Because I often work for weeks (sometimes months!) on a song, by the time it is done, it not only speaks to whatever it is about, but also captures that whole time I was figuring it out, shaping it and singing it as an accompaniment to our lives. A song not just describes, but recreates a whole season for us.

So I stretched the recording of these songs out over many months, enjoying the retreat the work provided. This would be my fourth album recorded in a studio, but the songs excited me in a way none of my other recordings had. Perhaps it was because these songs were more personal and more emotional than my previous work. This was my first batch of songs since becoming a father, after all. But much of the excitement, I believe, had to do with Corsica. Recording the songs brought it all back—the bells, those mountains, that little car, the language, the smell in the breeze, the quiet.

Not all the songs on the album came to me on that island. Somehow, though written in a very foreign part of the world, the Corsican songs seemed tied to several I had written before we left. Regardless of where they were set (Corsica, Glasgow, Brooklyn, a road back to Massachusetts), they all seemed to deal with slants on the same basic themes, themes I thought a lot about while living on the island: fatherhood, alienation, longing for home, nostalgia, salvation through love and family, and cures—what can pull you back from the edge and restore your hope.

***

Art should always be a living thing. One of the beauties of music is that musicians get to perform their songs anew again and again, thus recreating them every night. There's that famous recording of Joni Mitchell where she jokes about asking Van Gogh to paint "Starry Night" again. It's a ridiculous notion. But musicians get to do that. I get to do that. And when I sing a song again, I pretty much never think about what I felt when I wrote it. I think about how it relates to my world, or the worlds of the audience in front of me, right at that moment. And that's what that song means on that given night. Even for me, my songs shift and bend.

Still these songs all arose out of particular circumstances, were inspired by particular swirls of emotions, were attempts at expressing a certain set of thoughts and feelings. I like to set up my songs with stories when I perform them onstage, stories that aim to make people laugh, stories that relate to the lyrics, stories about how the songs came to be. As I was recording *Some Kind of Cure*, I realized I had stories to tell about so many of the songs. So during breaks in the studio or backstage at concerts, when my kids were napping or had gone to sleep for the night, I went through my journals from Corsica and Brooklyn and wrote this book.

What follows are thirteen short essays, they are the founding stories for each song on *Some Kind of Cure*. I have sequenced the stories in a different order than the songs on the album. I considered primarily chronology, settings and plot instead of instrumentation, key, tempo or lyrics. The book is divided into three sections based on where the songs were written: two "Corsica" sections bookend an "Elsewhere" section. The idea is that you read the stories, stopping after each to listen to the corresponding song. I hope they enhance each other, that the music informs the stories and the stories inform the music.

That being said, I certainly don't believe you need to read a book about or by a singer to understand what he sings about. A song may be mine as I write it, as I sing it, as I record it, but it also belongs to my wife, my children and my neighbors who hear it through the walls and down the road. It is yours as you listen to it, as you play it again, as you sing it. It is ours as we sing it together or listen to it together. I assume most artists and writers feel the same way. I care about what I write about, and all of my lyrics mean something deep and specific to me, but I am excited not frustrated if a listener has a totally different interpretation of a song. I am honored if a lyric can reshape itself to be relevant to someone else and her particular world. That feels like the point. That's what makes art more than just a selfish pursuit.

So I've tried to give enough without giving too much. I hope reading about certain people and situations that led to songs, and learning more about my feelings when I was writing the music, will not stop you from making it yours. Ultimately that is what I want, for these songs to be yours.

I. CORSICA

Venaco in the snow.

RINGING BELLS
AND SORCERERS

"Some Kind of Cure"

"Some Kind of Cure," the album's title track, begins with the ringing of a bell. That bell sits atop an old church in a very old village. That village is perched atop a hill surrounded by mountains in the heart of Corsica. If you'd like to visit, I suggest taking the high-speed ferry from the west coast of Italy or the French Riviera through the Mediterranean Sea (about a six-hour trip) until you reach the reluctantly French island. Then drive a couple hard hours into the mountains on a winding two-lane road keeping your eyes out for goats and aggressive drivers. Just before you reach the citadel of Corte, you'll see a bullet-dented white and black sign on your left pointing you toward an even smaller road. Go slow around switchback after switchback until the outline of the ancient stone houses and the church appears.

If you listen closely to the next few seconds of the song, you'll hear the voices and laughter of children playing in the little village square. They are out there without fail when the weather is nice, running around chasing balls and scraping their knees. Their fathers and grandfathers sit on the stone wall wearing casquettes or play Boules on the uneven pitch. Mothers and grandmothers cluster in the shade under wider hats or walk arm in arm along the winding road to the next village beyond the next hill.

That bell on that church rang everyday at noon and at six. No exception. Never late. But how long it rang was anyone's guess. There was no logic (at least that I managed to figure out) behind the number of times it rang—sometimes four, sometimes closer to twenty-four. Sometimes the wind blew so hard the bell would knock against the clapper long after it otherwise would have stopped ringing. I came to love the reliability of that bell and the way it divided our days, told us when to eat lunch, when to stop work, when to pour an aperitif and begin preparing dinner. I also came to love the mystery of that ringing bell, almost as if it had a mood of its own.

***

We actually lived in two different villages over the course of our year. The first was Venaco. We were there during the coldest months, and I remember it that way: cold and dark, both physically and culturally. We only stayed there for two months, but it felt a lot longer. I set up a small studio in the corner of our bedroom. The ceilings were so low I had to sit down to play and sing. My microphone was beside a window that opened onto tiled red roofs and folds upon folds of mountains.

That house was up a seemingly undriveable hill. We were afraid whenever Jackson would toddle out of the door that he would tumble down the road and off a cliff. The house had old exposed beams and a tiny iron fireplace. There were three small floors and a tight set of stairs that connected each. Jackson did in fact fall, though not off a cliff. He tumbled down one of the flights of stairs and gashed open his cheek, which (along with the dark and the cold) prompted us to look for a new home. Given village politics, that was only possible if the new home was also in a new village.

***

When we first discovered the village that would be ours for the rest of the year, it appeared as if from some book of fairy tales. This was Tralonca, and it was set in the mountains up a road so narrow and winding that we initially ruled it out as a possible place to live. We found it after a light snow had fallen, so the beige stone walls and red roofs were almost sparkling. Because of the snow and the setting, the village was majestic. But it was also crumbling and leaning against itself, not at all like some gleaming castle in the distance. It was weird and gnarled, with secret paths and hidden alleyways, a cobbled together sort of a place, something out of a child's imagination or an old faded postcard that had been folded a few too many times.

We lived in two different houses in Tralonca. Sarah's favorite was smaller, with ceilings just higher than my head and wooden doorframes that were just lower than my head. It got great light in the mornings and had a small table with two white iron chairs outside the front door. The kitchen was full of French things, foreign things that wouldn't be in a basic American kitchen: little porcelain hard-boiled-egg cups, small espresso mugs with tiny handles, brown ceramic yogurt pots that we used as cups for afternoon coffee, a crock pot. There was a baguette, fresh clementines in a wooden bowl and a heavily starched pile of linen waiting for us when we moved in. Our bedroom had a long view of distant hills and little terraced farms below our window where the men in our village grew their courgettes and haricot verts. We would hear them working the land and talking to one another in the early mornings. There was a great cross breeze in that apartment when the windows were open that kept Sarah content.

Our other place, which we called "la grande house," was my favorite. It had a large open fireplace that I tended to nightly and a wide terrace where we hung our laundry and ate our meals, weather permitting. Our bedroom windows were French doors that opened onto a tiny balcony right beside the old church and its bell. We faced the mountains and the one "commercial establishment" in the village—a family bar that was only open when the family was home and wanted to open it. Even then it seemed only open to the owner's friends and family (of which we became both, in a sense, by the end of our year). "It's just like some guy with a big liquor cabinet," Sarah said early on. "Every once in a while he invites you in for a drink, and then sometimes he charges you."

I swept out the fireplace in the mornings, collecting the ashes in a bucket, which I then carried down the stone steps from our home and over to the wall that held our town in against the mountain. I threw the ashes over the edge and watched them swirl and blow down, sometimes back into my face, and sometimes out and away across the hillside. I liked to imagine they traveled clear across Corsica and then out into that mythic sea, which though not often in sight, was rising and falling at all moments around every inch of our old island.

***

Corsicans are very superstitious. They believe that certain people can curse you with what they call the "evil eye." Some hold charms in their pockets or on chains around their necks to ward it off. They believe in sorcerers. Sarah actually met a man claiming to be a sorcerer while she was hiking alone in a canyon. She had been walking for several miles and had strayed off the trail to get down to the river. An old man appeared out of nowhere. He was walking down from the higher mountains through the middle of the shallow current. He offered her some of his baguette, showed her an old book of mysterious writings, and then walked away and disappeared. Things like this happen over there.

We heard a lot about charms and beliefs when we first arrived, things we should or shouldn't say or do. When a bad thing happens to someone, it is presumed that someone else brought on that bad luck. After much went wrong in our village and people talked about what a hard year it had been for them, we worried they thought we had brought the curse.

We didn't sleep well in the beginning. Maybe it was how our house in the first village was perched on the side of the mountain; it felt like our beds might slide down the hill. Maybe it was the quiet. Coming from Brooklyn, that quiet took a lot of getting used to. Or maybe it was some sort of black magic. Corsicans don't like outsiders, and maybe they had put a hex on us.

Jackson had the hardest time sleeping. Night terrors it seemed. He cried and cried. We would wait as long as we could, noiselessly hoping that the silence in between his wails meant he had fallen back to sleep. Inevitably, he'd start crying again. We would give in and go to him, lifting him out of his crib and into our arms. He was often inconsolable. We rocked him and held him tightly and sang to him. But he seemed in a sort of altered state. We tried everything to calm him, but he frequently worked himself into hysterics before we could finally get him back to bed.

You always think the sound of your child's cry is louder than it is, but we had no doubt Jackson was waking up the entire village. The houses were so tightly packed, stacked and folded in on themselves like Tetris pieces. We shared all sorts of walls with our old neighbors. The villagers seemed critical of so many things about us, and Jackson's sleep troubles no doubt were high on their lists.

With Jackson screaming in those dark cold nights, not a single other fluent English speaker it seemed within a thousand miles, and no family or friends to call on, things felt quite out of control, and it was hard not to question the rationale behind our move. It felt like maybe we had made a big mistake by dragging our innocent child all the way across the world. Time was moving very slowly, and it seemed like we were in for a really long and frightening year. The sensation was strange. The beauty around us was so tremendous, and yet in the beginning we couldn't seem to see it, to let it take over. I began to hear a melody in my head. The lyric I started mumbling was, "Corsica, I'm calling from over here." Although I wasn't sure to whom I was calling, it felt like a call for help.

***

Unlike the bell in Tralonca, the bell in Venaco rang on the hour. Every hour. It didn't even stop at night. I couldn't believe it at first. Why would anyone want a bell to ring on the hour all night long? It was yet another thing that kept us awake in the beginning. Eventually the ringing became a calming force and we slept through it. If we did hear it, the sound began to feel somehow reassuring, as if someone was up making sure all was okay. Time was still moving like it was supposed to move. Even if things didn't get better, we were only going to be there for a year, and this year would end.

One morning just before dawn, I awoke to that bell. It rang longer than normal. In fact it seemed like it had already been ringing for quite some time, all night maybe. Finally I got up, thinking something must be wrong. Had someone died? Was there some kind of emergency?

Sarah slept on. I crept downstairs as if possessed by the bell. I grabbed a hat, tied on a scarf and went out into the dark morning. All shutters were closed. All chimneys were pouring out lines of smoke. Everything was still and dark except these white streams of smoke in the black sky. The stars were electric. I had never seen so many stars. And there wasn't a sound. Except for that bell, which kept ringing and ringing. I walked toward the church, my pace increasing, the bell getting louder. I was the only one out, which surprised me because the ringing was so insistent. I kept expecting people to come out of their houses, to join me in this weird march. But no one did. I walked on alone.

My eyes got used to the dark, and I could make out the swinging bell up in the tower. I got to the church and tried the front door. Locked. I walked around to the back. That door was locked as well. The lights were off. There wasn't a sign of anyone, and I certainly didn't knock. My French wasn't good enough to ask any questions should someone happen to answer. I pictured some bent-nosed Corsican hunchback up there alone in the cold tower swinging that old bell like a madman.

I sat for a few minutes on the church steps wondering how I had gotten to where I sat, wondering what was going on, amazed by how far away the world I knew was, how helpless I was without language, how mysterious things seemed. Then I walked back home, the bell still ringing, echoing now off the distant mountains, creating the sensation that another bell was ringing in another distant village.

***

On the other side of the mountains where our village sat was the Corsican coast, and all along it are crumbling Genoese towers. They are shaped like rooks on a chessboard, single stone columns with tooth-like rims at the top. They stand mostly broken now, some falling into the sea. But back in the day, legend says, they were the first line of Corsican defense. Whenever the island was attacked, which it was often in its early history, someone would run to the top of the tower and light a fire. From the top of each tower, a watchman could see the tower to the north and the one to the south. When smoke rose from one, men would light flames atop their towers, and so on and so on, until every turret along the entire coast was ablaze. When the people saw the smoke they would retreat into the interior, into the wildly overgrown brush called "the maquis" and into the inner mountain villages, villages like ours.

Bells, I figured, could work just like smoke. One church rings its bell. The next village hears it and starts ringing its bell. Pretty soon, the entire island, all the peaks and pockets in the mountains, would be ringing and echoing, and everyone would hear the sound and know to hide.

The thought of an island-wide alarm spooked me, so when I got back home I went right in to check on Jackson. Still sleeping. Given his sleep troubles, I was relieved and a little surprised the ringing bell hadn't bothered him. He looked so peaceful and perfect, so safe. I crept back into my warm bed. Sarah, too, was still asleep. Amazing, I thought. How do they do it? My body was cold, and it felt good to get under the covers and feel her body beside mine. I sensed this profound contrast between the sound of their breathing and the cold and eerie ringing outside.

***

I never found out why the bell was ringing, and eventually I kind of stopped believing that it had happened in the first place. I chalked it up to some strange Corsican voodoo. But I continued to be haunted by this vision: I wake up and Sarah isn't beside me. I wander the cold, dark and still foreign house. I find her sitting at the kitchen table crying. I don't know why. There's nothing I can do. Has something terrible happened? I can't get to where she sits. The table is too long. The kitchen is too big. She's sadder than I want to believe. Whatever is wrong is bigger than I knew, too big for me to make better. It's a terrible vision. While she's at that table crying, this damn bell is ringing. I don't know why it's ringing. Is it for the same thing she's crying about? Is it something else? Or does it just happen to be ringing, for no reason at all? I'm not sure which is worse, which option more frightening.

In this nightmare, I'm desperate to make things better and I don't know how to do it, I don't know what I can do. I recall that strange sorcerer Sarah had met in the mountains. With no one to turn to, no family, no friends, no one who understands, I find myself wishing for some kind of sorcery to make it better, to keep us safe. I call out for some kind of cure. I hear my call echo off the mountains like the bell. "Oh sorceress, come conjure up some kind of cure." I regret the plea immediately when it leaves my lips. It feels like I'm proposing a deal with the devil.

***

No sorceress came. I don't believe in that kind of magic. But we were ultimately cured. What ended up saving us, what ended up helping us to make it through

29

our year, was something less mystical but no less profound. We resolved to believe in ourselves and each other, to let the strength of our little family sustain and preserve us in this strange place. And Sarah and I did actually make resolutions, sitting down at our kitchen table after Jackson finally fell asleep one January night. We resolved to be stronger than the world around us, not to let it swallow us up. We resolved to let the sights and sounds and tastes and smells of that stunning place wash over us without washing us away. We resolved to wander through that place and that time without losing ourselves or each other. In the end, that's the cure we were really calling for all along. And we were the only ones capable of conjuring it.

(*Play "Some Kind of Cure" now.*)

SOME KIND OF CURE

In the morning,
Bells kept ringing.
You were calling.
No one's listening.

And no one knew the reason why.
No one knew the reason why they rang.

At the table,
You were crying.
I was unsure
How to reach you.

You opened up your arms,
Opened up your arms to let me in.

Corsica, I'm calling from over here.
Oh sorceress, come conjure up some kind of cure.

Please hold me like you used to, baby.
Hold me like you would.
Please hold me like you know what I'm going through.

Some have told us,
Keep your distance.
There are secrets
That we keep here.

And that's as close as you will get.
That's as close as you will ever get.

Corsica, I'm calling from over here.
It's dangerous to open up more and more.
So sorceress, come conjure up some kind of cure.

Please hold me like you used to, baby.
Hold me like you would.
Please hold me like you know what I'm going through.
Hold me like you used to, baby.
Hold me like you would.
Please hold me like you know what I'm going through.

FETCHING WOOD
WITH FRANÇOIS

"All those Ashes"

Shortly after we arrived on Corsica, we were driving into the mountain town of Corte over a little bridge that crossed a swift and cold river. Sarah often conducted interviews at the small university there, and I worked a lot sitting on the big stones beside that river. As we drove across the bridge, we noticed a cluster of people looking over the edge. Men were running around frantically pointing down into the water. We pulled our car half onto the curb, flashers blinking and sprinted over to see what was happening. Apparently a woman in a black sweat suit had thrown herself off the bridge, an attempted suicide. She was bouncing against the rocks below. Three men had run down the steep bank and were reaching for her with long sticks from the shore. After being pulled under a couple terrifying times, she finally swirled into an eddy, and they managed to get her out. She suffered badly from shock but survived.

The scene hit us hard, and the image of her in that water stayed with me. Although Corsica was certainly civilized, there was something that still felt lawless and wild there. I had never before seen such narrow winding roads and such deadly drops without any barriers. The news was filled through our year with strange stories of people getting injured or dying. There were rockslides, mudslides, huge floods and storms. People drove over cliffs. People drowned. Anything we did, adventures and events that might otherwise have just been interesting or exciting, was often tinged with at least a measure of fear. For much of the year, I was more aware of my mortality than I was accustomed to.

***

One night in February, there was an unusually large storm that dumped over a foot of wet snow on our village and knocked out the electricity. I woke up to an incredibly dark house and sky. Jackson awoke soon after, scared by the darkness and unable to go back to sleep. I took him downstairs. We pulled up a big chair beside the double glass doors to see what we could see. The house was cold, as the heat was out, so I pulled a blanket over us. The stove didn't work either, so we ate yogurt and waited for it to get lighter. It was still snowing and snowing hard when the day finally dawned. We were of course snowed in, as our mountain road was impassable in a hard rain let alone a big blizzard. Our tiny car was buried. Icicles soon clung to the village roofs, some as long as four or five feet.

Sarah was more worried than I was about the state of things. I had some wood for the fire, which had fast become an obsession of mine. We had hats and scarves. And the snow was beautiful. We bundled up in sweaters and read stories. It was all quite romantic for a few hours with the snow still coming down. But by mid morning, power still out, I got a bit stir crazy and did an inventory of our food supply. My mood began to change. If our road wasn't plowed, I figured we might be stranded for a couple days. When I saw how little was in our cupboard, I began to think more soberly about our situation up there on the mountain.

The chances of anyone clearing the tiny road to Tralonca were slim at best. We had to be a pretty low priority on the Corsican road map. Even the few larger streets on the island would likely take a while to clear. I had never really seen the local government on top of any maintenance problems (pot holes, rock slides, etc.). When work got done, it was often a friend or a guy from your village who, fed up with whatever was wrong, decided to round up a few of his cousins, throw on some gloves and boots and repair a patch of road or a fence himself. There were rarely cones out when there were workmen on a scene. You didn't see safety vests, flashing lights or anything official. When drivers would pass these "work crews," many would stop to talk, probably thanking them for finally taking matters into their own hands, maybe inviting them over for dinner or a drink when they finished up.

***

Most of our wood was gone by around noon, and the snow was still coming down. So when our next-door neighbor François came by to see if I wanted to go with him to fetch some logs, I was more than a little relieved. François was from mainland France and not Corsica, a distinction that was a big deal on the island. Unlike most of the continental French who look way down their noses on Corsicans, François worshiped them like noble savages. He was, according to some sarcastic comments from villagers, "more Corsican than even the Corsicans." And, in fact, it did seem that way. He wore fatigues, smoked a lot of hand-rolled cigarettes, carried a gun, kept chickens and rabbits in a little hut down the hill, drove a motorcycle and loved to talk about killing wild boar with a knife. He also lived somewhat of a bandit-like existence, moving with his family four different times during the single year we knew him and even abandoning a car loaded with his stuff on the side of our village road for about six months until a few of our neighbors grew tired of seeing it and decided to push it down the hill.

I am obviously not Corsican either. But unlike François, I don't smoke, I can't stand guns, and I've never killed anything in my life—certainly not with a knife— and I hope I never have to. Machismo is a big deal in all Mediterranean cultures, Corsica's for sure. My role as musician, primary caretaker of a child, chief shopper and chef in the family did not exactly help to win me a cowboy image with the town folk. Nor did it help that I was only on the island in the first place to support my wife's work. So I had an ulterior motive when François came knocking—get fuel for the fire, for sure, but also let a few neighbors see my rugged side as I braved the blizzard to provide for my family.

I said yes to François and the expedition began before I realized a few things. First, I had nothing in the way of gear—no gloves, no boots, nothing waterproof. Second, fetching wood with François also meant bringing along two big bags of food scraps from the restaurant where he worked so we could feed the chickens and rabbits he kept on the side of the mountain. Third, and most significantly, I would have to carry François' rifle (because he started out with both bags of food) in the hope that we would find (and I would kill) a certain fox that kept getting into his chickens.

I tried to play it cool as he handed me the fun. But the truth is, as far as I could recall, I had never in my life held a gun before, certainly not one that was loaded. It was heavy and awkward. The last time I had held anything even close was in a preschool performance of Peter and the Wolf. I was maybe four and got to carry a plastic popgun over my shoulder. I didn't know if I should hold this gun like I had in the play or hold it down as I would if I were carrying a pair of scissors. Or should I take aim, walking with it in ready position like Elmer Fudd, waiting and wanting to shoot at anything that moved?

We trudged through waist-deep drifts, up a slope, over partially buried walls, through a break in an old fence, falling at times, me afraid I might myself, and François stumbling and spilling rotten cabbages and stale bread out across the snow. My whole lower half quickly became wet and freezing cold. I had a hard time keeping up with François. He was a man in his element, or at least he was putting on a good show. There was a wild look in his eyes, sort of fox-like himself. He'd laugh, throw his head back and yodel as he ran through the snow, encouraging me with French expressions I didn't understand.

We eventually made it to the coop. The rabbits were easy. They were docile and confined in mesh cages. It was dark in there and they didn't bother us. Chickens, on the other hand, are a little friskier, a more independent-minded species. Even François, with his fatigues, seemed a bit uneasy about the loud clucking of the birds we heard coming from behind the big rough board that blocked the entrance. They hadn't been fed in a couple days I learned, and they could get pretty aggressive when hungry.

The board was tied in place with little ropes hooked onto nails on either side and held back by four large stones. François slowly rolled away the stones one by one, while I pressed against the wood with my foot and shoulder. I could feel the birds' bodies banging up against the board. They were really hollering at this point, and I couldn't imagine how we were going to move the wood out of the way without twenty birds erupting into our faces. François was clearly concerned now as well, nervously laughing in my direction. But they had to be fed. So as I flinched, he undid the coils of rope. With a deep breath and his head turned away, he pulled aside the board and released the flock.

It went far better than we expected. In fact looking back on it now, it was sort of a let down. Following François' lead, we both let out a sort of war cry and ran into the dark room with arms waving. The birds, on the other hand, barely reacted at all, making our behavior seem pretty ridiculous. They just continued strutting, having little interest in us and no interest in getting near the cold wind and snow. François chuckled and shrugged his shoulders at me. We made fast work of it, dumping the old vegetables into the trough and scooping up several fists of snow into a pail for them to drink. Then François closed the door and hooked the ropes back. I secured the stones, and we were on our way.

Luckily we saw no sign of the fox, for I still had the gun. If it had appeared, I suppose I would have had to shoot. I was pretty sure that would not have gone well. I'd been worried about the possibility the entire time. How much resistance was there in the trigger? Would I need more than a single finger to pull it? It probably would have sent me flying backward into the snow, probably dislocating a shoulder. And I really stood no chance of hitting the animal, particularly not unless someone else had hit it first. I likely would have killed one of the chickens. I might even have killed François.

We started back, now looking out for wood, the original purpose of the expedition. I could see nothing burnable in sight. Everything was white. François kept stopping in the blowing snow. He'd put his arm over my shoulder and pull me close. Bringing his face right next to mine, he'd say in his odd mixture of French and English, how beautiful it was. And it really was beautiful. Incredibly so. Perfectly quiet. No one in sight. Cold and clear with snow stretching as far as we could see up into the mountains, blanketing the red roofs of our village. There was total stillness except the blowing wind. The trees creaked softly under thick cover. And there we were: two solitary men on the side of a mountain, talking about beauty with barely any words in common.

In the middle of our awkward dialogue, François disappeared up a snow bank to our right. I followed, tripping over a buried stone wall. Somehow in all this white, François had found a big stash of wood, a small darkish hump rising just barely out of the snow. We gathered as much as our bags could hold. François then threw a huge stump over his back, and we descended—

back over that stone wall, back down the slope, back through the fence, and then back through the waist-deep drifts to find our road and our homes.

It was really hard going with the weight of the wood, the rifle, the tired legs and all. Even François was struggling, panting hard. At times I thought I might not be able to go on, that François would have to go on without me and get help. But I made it out. Then I spent much of the next hour trying to set the wet wood ablaze—using all but three of our matches. Remembering the Jack London Story, "To Build a Fire," I swallowed my pride and enlisted Sarah to help me get it going. We heated up a lunch of corn and pizza slices in a little pan, which we managed to hook on a stick over the fire. The snow was no longer falling but had blown into impressive drifts against the church wall and in the alley leading to our house. I felt pretty good about the mission as I boasted about it to Sarah and Jackson. Mostly I was relieved that I didn't have to shoot that gun. Sarah reminded me, though, that despite it all, we still only had enough wood to maybe get us through the night. With the amount of snow out there, we weren't sure that would be enough.

A couple cozy hours passed, and then it started to snow again. So with prodding from Sarah (and cheers from Jackson) I headed back out there to look for more wood. This would be a solo search, as François was now busy hauling out a huge generator from lord knows where. He waved some tube excitedly in my direction, miming that he planned to siphon gas out of a few of the villagers' cars to power the thing. I gave him an awkward thumbs up and then climbed back out into the snow looking for our tracks, which now were mostly buried.

I thought I remembered the basic path, but about five minutes in and chest-deep in a drift, I realized I had no idea where I was going. I could still see our village, so I wasn't worried about getting lost. But I was having a hard time moving, getting closer and closer to stuck with every labored step. I imagined the scene. François high on siphoned gas fumes, his generator now powering his house. And me, out there again, stuck in the snow about ten meters from the road, completely unable to move. I wondered what I would yell, or if they'd even hear. When would it be that Sarah or the villagers might come looking for me? What a sight they would find: the dead American, frozen solid, only steps from his home.

It didn't happen. I managed to get loose and found a couple more pieces of wet wood sticking out of the snow and clawed my way back home. The power kicked back on maybe 45 minutes later (just as François got his generator going). We made hot chocolate, heated up some soup on the stovetop and drank cold beer.

The snow stopped overnight. The new day broke thick with fog—as the air was warm and the ground still frozen. We built a large snowman topped with Jackson's camouflage cap to make him appear Corsican. Sarah shoveled our patio and the steps down to the square. And then around mid-morning, a plow came. Everyone was surprised to see it, until the driver waived and we saw that it was one of our neighbors at the wheel.

***

Without power and a cleared road for merely a single day, the alarm and the near fatal missions for wood seemed perhaps a tiny bit excessive. I tried to play it cool, like I hadn't ever been worried. But the truth is that I was worried. It was a humbling lesson on how limited my skill set was should I ever really have to go native and provide for my family.

There were a lot of ashes to get rid of the next morning from all the wood we had burned. I filled a big bag and carried it down with Jackson to the edge of our village square. Together we threw the ashes out over the wall, out over the snow in the direction of François' chickens. The wind picked the ashes up immediately and blew them around over the crusted snow in a swirling pattern that looked almost like a dark, fast moving river.

The image of that woman who had thrown herself into the river came back to me then. The black of the ashes on the snow swirling away from us was a lot like that lady's dark form out of control in the water. I had thought about her many times since that day, had even started working on a song. It wasn't really about suicide, but about the course of a life, about getting older and ultimately about dying naturally, without regret, when the time came. I populated the lyrics with images from our world there—chestnut trees, clothes on the clothesline. I tried to draw a quick sketch of Sarah's and my life together—from her crooked grin that I noticed upon first falling for her, to the spools of thread she'd used making clothes in the little shop she opened in the East Village, from me on my knees proposing, to my leaving too often to go on tour. I tried to have the song move and flow like a river.

I wondered if that woman had any family to comfort her after she threw herself into the water. What did she tell them? What did they say? I reached for Jackson's hand. We walked back up to our house slowly, Jackson thrilled by the snow and thinking about little else other than how much he could grab and put into his small mouth. I was having heavier thoughts, about how fragile a life can be, about how much we needed to look out for each other.

There was something that seemed so right about those ashes blowing away out over the snow, both chaotic and yet perfectly patterned as they were taken by the wind currents. In that moment it seemed that wildness was the natural state of things. All the structure we create around us is just that, a creation, and things can dissolve back into disorder so quickly. Big pieces of heavy wood were now just ashes blowing around.

I started thinking about getting older myself, about the disorder that aging would bring. There was something very unnatural about that woman in that river. That was not the way we were meant to die. But death itself wasn't unnatural, and getting older wasn't unnatural, as hard as we try to resist both.

I scooped Jackson up into my arms and ruffled his hair and shook off the thoughts. Then I opened the door into our warm, well-lit house feeling quite lucky to be held by the two of them and to have them to hold. I scribbled down a line about ashes floating in a river. "Rock me river, rock me slow, take me where I'm meant to go, with all those ashes floating slow."

(*Play "All those Ashes" now.*)

ALL THOSE ASHES

Hold me river,
Here's my bones.
Look at all those river stones
Forming patterns on the shore
Of the man I was before.

Clothes now dripping off the line.
Stubborn sun don't want to shine.
If I could turn it back, don't know,
Don't know what I'd forego.

She's the girl with the crooked grin,
Thoughts all waiting to begin.
She's the one with the spools of thread,
Colors always in her head.

And I'm the boy in the chestnut trees.
I'm the boy still on his knees.
I'm the one in the crumpled clothes.
I'm the boy who comes and goes.

Oh no. Oh no. Oh no.
And oh, momma I'm fine.
Don't worry all the time.
Don't worry all the time.

And oh, that fire burned so fast.
Promises they couldn't last.
Pictures in those wooden frames,
Faces now don't look the same.

And all the lessons that we learned,
All of that too quickly burned,
In the river down below,
All those ashes floated slow.

Oh no. Oh no. Oh no.
And oh, momma I'm fine.
Don't worry all the time.
I'm coming home.
Sweet river take me home.
Sweet river take me home.
Sweet river take me home.

Rock me river, here I am.
Come on take me back again.
Rock me river, rock me slow.
Take me where I'm meant to go.
With all those ashes floating slow.
With all those ashes floating slow.
With all those ashes floating slow.
All those ashes.

Sarah taking clothes off the line outside our window in Venaco.

HOW TO USE AN AXE

"Hope for Better Days"

I came to believe that smoke rising from a chimney was a sign of virility on the island. The measure of my manliness was gauged each winter night by how high and for how long smoke rose from our roof.

During the day, we could see our neighbors watching us. But I believe they must have taken shifts at night, little wrinkled faces peeping out on the half-hour from behind otherwise tightly closed shutters. And what did they find coming from our chimney? On most nights, not a whole lot.

That wasn't entirely true. I made plenty of fires, particularly when we moved to Tralonca. In Venaco, though, most died out shortly after I went to bed. And that was fine. The place had heat after all, as did all the houses in the village. The need for fire was a symbolic one now. Still that didn't temper the pressure on me to keep the flames going or quiet the talking behind our backs when I didn't.

The fireplace in our first house wasn't large. It was more like a little oven with a small metal door that sealed it shut. You could see the glow through a little soot-stained window. Not exactly the vision of a cozy hearth. It didn't draw very well, and we didn't have much in the way of tools. In fact, the only thing resembling a bellows was a barbecue gizmo I found in some drawer meant to help light charcoal. It had a four-inch plastic tube with a small peg that rotated a little flywheel. It made a whirring noise when you turned it, puffing out a small asthmatic current of air. It looked like a child's toy, something you might get for a couple tickets won playing Ski Ball.

So I would pull open the iron door and get right up to the fire, whizzing that tiny handle around between two fingertips to help grow the flames. I had to get very close to the coals, as the tube wasn't very long, and in the process my face got dangerously hot. I'd turn away when I couldn't stand it any longer with a wildness in my eyes that frightened my family.

If I did get the fire going, it was nearly impossible to sustain it while we slept. When I awoke in the middle of the night, I would force myself to get up, stumble down the stairs and check to see if there were any coals still glowing. If so, I'd shove another piece of wood in and stumble back up to bed. I would have been content to just let the fire burn out, if not for all those critical eyes. Every morning, "t'as illuminé le feu?" the neighbors asked me, knowing damn well the answer. And I'd lie, "oui, oui. Bien sur." Then I'd wave and walk away from them as fast as I could.

***

One morning in January, I heard a loud banging outside our door. I peeked out, and there was our old neighbor Dumé chopping wood with his brother in-law, Jacques. Jacques had to be in his seventies, with a full head of silver hair. But he was in remarkable shape. He still worked as a wilderness guide, taking people up into the high mountains. Dumé, on the other hand, was small and somewhat fragile looking. He appeared old enough to almost be Jacques' father. He must have been in his late eighties. Hardly five-feet tall, he wore turtlenecks tucked into his jeans, which were always pulled up quite high. His head had just a handful of white wisps over the top and seemed too large for his body, an impression that the turtlenecks only enhanced.

Though he lived above us, until that day, Dumé and I had said very little to each other. He spoke no English. I spoke virtually no French. What he did say was either in Corsican or a French so heavily accented that even if I had known the vocabulary I wouldn't have been able to make it out.

Pretty much our entire relationship revolved around the weather. He'd tell me "il pleut," when it was raining.

I'd guess at what he'd said and then smile and agree. "Oui, Dumé. Il pleut." Later the same day, assuming it was still raining, he'd tell me again, as if for the first time. I'd agree again.

Dumé seemed to always be around when we went in or out of our house. He would find small tasks that gave him an excuse to pass by our door or open window. He'd walk slowly and carefully with a single can of beans, a small piece of wood or maybe a screwdriver to the basement, which brought him by our little parking place and kitchen window. A few minutes later we'd see him return, often with the same item still in his hands. He didn't have much to do, and Americans living next door might well have been the biggest deal in his last thirty years.

Suddenly, as I'd be peeling potatoes or making coffee, I'd see an umbrella and then his large bald head pop up just outside our open window.

"Il pleut, Dahveed!"

"Oui, Dumé. Il pleut."

Given his age and general level of activity, I was a little surprised on that cold morning to see Dumé, axe in hand, out in the field with Jacques, a huge pile of logs beside them. They were trading blows, cutting the wood into kindling. I hadn't used as much of the wood from the pile beside our house as many of the villagers might have liked, but I certainly had used some of it. I had wondered each time I took a piece for our fire if it was definitely mine to take. The pile leaned against a wall shared by several flats, and no one had explicitly told me that I could take from it. I didn't know where the wood came from or if I was expected to replenish it. So I was glad to see them out chopping, and I rushed to find a hat and coat so I could lend a hand.

It took them a while to get that I was offering to help. This was due both to my lack of language and because

I don't think they believed I would actually be able to chop wood. I pantomimed a bit to help them get what I was trying to say, pointing to the pile and to the axe. I patted myself on the chest and then demonstrated my best woodcutting motion. I hadn't chopped wood in years (if ever), and I suppose my pantomiming was pretty poor, because they just nodded politely and then went on with their work. Finally, I ran back inside and got Sarah to come out and talk for me (which I had to do all the time during the year). This of course didn't help my reputation any, but it did help them understand what I was trying to say. They nodded in appreciation and then smiled to each other like they had some preexisting inside joke. Then Dumé handed me the axe.

"Here we go again," I thought to myself as I felt the axe. Just like the rifle I had been asked to carry, the axe was way to big for me. I don't think I showed it on my face, or at least I tried hard not to show it on my face, but I knew straight away, like when you pick a far too heavy bowling ball up off the rack, that there was very little chance I was going to be able to make it do what it was meant to do. If I did manage to somehow hoist the blade up and over my shoulder, there was no telling where it (or I) might fall.

I had watched Jacques and Dumé, in turns, handling the axe with such ease and grace. They manipulated it like a fly rod or a baton. It was beautiful in a way. They tossed the axe high up into the air. Their hands slid smoothly along the weathered oak handle. The silver blade flashed in the winter sun and down it sliced directly into the center of each frozen chunk of wood. One fluid motion, with seemingly no effort, no tension, no kinks. The logs divided into equal portions. Sometimes two. Sometimes three or four. And the pieces splayed out from the center like a fistful of pick-up sticks.

So that was how it was done. That was their expectation. And that's what I was trying to envision when they set a hunk of tree on its end and handed me the huge wooden shaft, my arm dropping a bit under its weight. I grinned in their direction. With a "what the hell" thought in my head, I tried to hoist the big axe up and over my shoulder.

To my pleasant surprise, I managed to get it up. I teetered a moment at the apex, but I did manage to get the axe to come down on the correct side of me. Grunting loudly, I slammed the blade into the cold wood. The shock to my ungloved hands was tremendous. I felt it through both forearms, in my biceps, my jaw, even my temples. The effect on the wood, however, was not quite as tremendous. My eyes had closed when the axe crashed down, but as I opened them, like a quarterback who had been thrown to the ground while releasing a potential touchdown pass, I realized the blade had barely made a scratch into the frozen surface of the log. It may have worked an inch or so in, but it certainly didn't split the wood. "Oh crap," I thought to myself, rubbing my hands. "Oh crap. Oh crap." The two old men were laughing hard. I managed a grin and tried to let out a laugh.

I gave it a couple more quick goes. These efforts were not much better than my first. I still hadn't succeeded in chopping through this one log. Had they given me a trick piece? It felt like the thing might be petrified.

By this point, a gallery of sorts had emerged. I have no idea how word spread so quickly. But the American was out there with Dumé, and everyone seemed to know and, of course, wanted to watch. Many of our neighbors came out of their houses and were either huddling around the perimeter of the field or standing on their balconies, giving the scene a tournament sort of feel. I felt like a trapped bull. Under normal circumstances I might have enjoyed the attention or would have joked my way out. But I didn't have the language to be self-deprecating, so I had to just endure it and hope that my next attempt would go better. I could hear a lot of laughter now, and certain words poked out. I didn't understand most of them, but the words I did catch were not kind.

Surprisingly, the image of Gary Cooper playing Lou Gehrig in *The Pride of the Yankees* came to mind. There's a scene at a fair where he's trying to impress his girl by swinging a big hammer to get a ball to rise and hit a bell. He's pretty confident he'll win without much effort. He's a decent baseball player after all. But at first, he's all biceps, and the ball barely rises. The carnival man teaches him to loosen his wrists, and after a few swings, he's smacking that thing and wins his girl a huge stuffed bear.

Sarah and Jackson came out from our house at that point. I shot them a nervous smile, shrugged my shoulders and heaved up the axe. Now with supple wrists and the new pressure from all the spectators, I flung it and my body back down toward the same scuffed piece of wood. I hit it. And the hit was a hell of a lot harder than my first tries. But because of the new looseness, my aim was terrible. I just nicked the corner of the wood, slicing off a chip that flew straight at Dumé. The rest of the wood just tipped over in the other direction. Dumé dodged the chip with impressive and surprising agility for a man of his age.

"Doucement, Dahveed. Doucement," he said, taking the axe out of my hand and patting me on the shoulder in a great-grandfatherly sort of a way. There was more laughter and commentary now, from Dumé, from Jacques, from the gallery, from my wife and child.

I had only taken maybe a half-dozen swings, but it felt like my hands might never close again. With some nods and gestures, and a quick rub of my neck, Dumé tried to get me to relax. He adjusted where I positioned my hands, showed me how high to swing the blade and how my hands should flow as they fell. He chopped five or six in quick succession, much to the approval and pride of the whole village, who clapped and cheered, nodding their heads, pointing and talking among themselves. Then, though I was trying to slink away, he gave the axe back to me. When the first swing wasn't a lot better than my early attempts, most of the spectators gave up on me.

They returned to their houses shaking their heads and laughing. But I persisted, and Dumé was patient. After another couple tries, I started to get it down. I began envisioning the ground beneath the wood. I kept my eyes open. I didn't get so carried away by the upswing. Finally, much to my relief, the pieces began to fall.

Sarah and Jackson were still out there. So unlike most of the village, they saw me redeem myself, and they were proud. When all the wood had been cut, Dumé invited me and Jacques and a couple other old men into his house for some of his basement-made moonshine. It was so strong I could hardly swallow it. My hands and back were throbbing, my ego was wounded, and all these men were ribbing me and my country for my inability to chop wood. Later we looked back and laughed pretty hard about it all, but at the time, unable to respond, I just had to sit and take it. All I wanted was to get out of there.

***

For the next several days as I was nursing my calloused hands, this song about escape I had tried to write a long time ago came back to me. It was about leaving a trapped situation, about ignoring the negativity around you, about believing in better days to come. Like a lot of bits of melody and lyrics, I had given up on it. It wasn't personal enough. But of all places, in this mountain village on this island, with all those little old eyes bearing down on us, this promise of escape suddenly felt like exactly what I wanted. What I would have given to say "piss off," or its French equivalent, to my nosy neighbors and to return to a place where I wouldn't be judged based on my skills as a woodsman and fire starter, to take my little family and get away. I reworked the changes to the song and rewrote the words. I needed more lyrics for the chorus, and that night as I was stuffing my newly chopped wood into our little fireplace, a line about "hope for better days" came to mind.

Over the course of the year, the word "hope" became a rallying call for Obama's presidential campaign. Particularly in our first months abroad, the word resonated loudly—both because we were witnessing firsthand how much of the world had come to dislike America, and because the message spoke of transcendence and even escape.

Diversity is rarely looked on with curiosity in a tiny village, at least it wasn't in our tiny village. So, in the beginning, we were judged on everything we did—not only how awkward I was with an axe, but also when and what we ate for dinner, how much or how little we doted over Jackson, how infrequently we washed our sheets, how messy our kitchen was, what our beliefs were, what our government did. The list went on and on. And it didn't help that I couldn't explain myself. I made a staggering number of verbal faux pas (like mixing up *revendre* and *revenir* at Jackson's crèche, thus implying I would "resell" instead of "return for" my child). Being able to say (and have people understand) any utterance—even something that was spelled the same in English and French was an accomplishment that might thrill me for the rest of the day. Most of the time, even just a slight error in emphasis or vowel sound would make what I was saying totally unintelligible to whomever I was speaking.

I'd like to say I wrote "Hope for Better Days" on Obama's victory night or perhaps sitting in a bar back in Atlanta the following January, seeing all those people across the Mall listening to his inauguration speech. But the truth is that I wrote it months before, on an island across the world, with a sore back, hurt pride and a pile of wood that, even though I had chopped it myself, I still couldn't manage to burn.

(Play "Hope for Better Days" now.)

HOPE FOR BETTER DAYS

Oh to disappear,
Board a fast plane
And never look their way.
We leave all of our fear,
All their warnings,
And all that's worn and frayed.
All we save is hope for better days.

It's all we have,
Hope for better days.
It's all we have.
It's all we need.

And when those lights appear,
When we crest the hill,
The city's in our eyes.
Hand upon the wheel,
And the pedal down,
Everything alive.
Through the evening sky, I hear them say.

It's on its way,
Hope for better days.
It's almost here.
So sing for me, now.
And I will sing for you.
Yeah, sing for me, now.
And I will sing for you.

And throwing your arm over my shoulder,
Believe me we pulled one over.
Leaving their world far behind.
And now, the lights are shining.

So sing for me, now.
And I will sing for you.
It's all we have.
Hope for better days.

Trying to chop wood. (Photo by Sarah Davis.)

140 GOATS AND THE SHIRTLESS SHEPHERD

"Homesick"

One day in early March, Jackson and I were called on to accompany Sarah on one of her countless anthropological excursions. We had been to the top of a lot of mountains—"pilgrimages" the Corsicans call them—to participate in outdoor masses in crumbling chapels. We had waited outside museums while Sarah was given tours, outside restaurants while she interviewed someone or other, outside churches while she took singing lessons. We had gone to see cheese makers and wood workers, had to put on shower caps and gloves in cellars where charcuterie makers cure their meat. We had endured long and tedious dinners so that Sarah could record conversations after the wine had set in and people talked loosely. I had managed to occupy and entertain Jackson in some of the most uncomfortable, steep, thorny, arid, child-unfriendly spots in the entire world. Our modus operandi was to never turn down an invitation and, unless absolutely necessary, to never leave early. This time we were going to find a shepherd.

The road to the shepherd's land was not really a road but rather a couple ruts in a boulder-strewn field. With every bumpy meter, I felt our chances of ever being able to drive back out dwindle. We found the correct route with the help of numerous townsfolk, asking where the shepherd lived (he didn't need a name). His place had no address, was not on a road at all, in fact. It was smack in the middle of a field. I pictured a guy like Moses, an old windblown man in a long white robe, full of face lines, with wild hair and a wilder beard. The man who emerged from his little shack when we finally found it, however, was several years younger than me and had close-cut hair. He was strong. He was handsome. And he was not wearing a shirt.

We gave the bisous, the traditional kiss on both cheeks, a custom practiced between two men as well. I got more used to this as the year went on but never quite got it right. Sometimes I planted my lips too squarely on the other man's cheek or too close to his mouth. Sometimes I let the stubble on our faces rub too much. And I never knew what I was supposed to do with my hands. The bisous was always at least a little awkward for me, and it was all the more awkward when one or both of us wasn't wearing a shirt.

After the shepherd and I kissed, he invited us into his place. It was a single room with no electricity. Dried meat and herbs hung from the walls. Flies circled a sticky fly strip. The couch in the corner he motioned me toward was an abandoned row of seats from a passenger van. He gave Jackson a box of juice and offered one to me. Jackson was delighted. I hadn't had a box of apple juice in quite some time, so I accepted as well. We poked our tiny straws through the tin foil-covered holes, and I took Jackson outside to see what we could see and let Sarah get to work.

The door to the shack had two swinging sections, upper and lower. Both closed abruptly behind us, leaving Sarah alone with the shirtless shepherd and leaving Jackson and me alone in a vast dusty field. We entertained ourselves for about thirty minutes or so with excitement, exploring the shelters where the goats were fed, climbing up and down on the big rocks. For a while we had a great time, running around and enjoying our juice. My only real challenge was stopping Jackson from eating what must have looked like thousands of little chocolates scattered all over the ground.

Eventually, though, the face of the shepherd emerged from behind the top half of his wooden door. He yodeled loudly, in Corsican I assumed, and within minutes 140 goats descended from the high hills. (This number was provided later; there were far too many for me to get a good count at the time.) Upon seeing them start to appear, the shepherd smiled at me. It was a strange sort of grin, a little mischievous I thought. I wasn't sure if it had to do with the descending goats or with the fact that he was in a small hut with my wife. Either way, he disappeared quickly, closing the door loudly behind him.

Jackson was thrilled. He had never seen so many goats. I had never seen so many goats. They were curious and frisky and let him pet them. It occurred to me in a semi-frightened flash, that I really didn't know the first thing about goats. I certainly didn't know anything about this breed of goats. Were they clean? I didn't know. Were they dangerous? No idea. Would they bite? Couldn't say. I didn't know the answers to any of these questions, but with my little son surrounded, just the fact I had started to even ask them at all seemed answer enough.

I needed to find a safe escape, and I needed to find it quickly and subtly, not wanting to transfer my goat anxiety onto Jackson. I weighed my choices. Sarah had the keys to the car, and I didn't think we could go back into the shack. What would I say? Mind if we pop in for another juice? Then I spotted the one raised feature in the landscape aside from the boulders, most of which had already been claimed by the bigger goats. It was a broken down blue Ford pickup. It seemed like my only possibility. I moved quickly, hoisting Jackson up and into the truck bed. I set him down and then climbed in after him, relieved, standing now as if on an altar above a sea of goats.

For a moment there was something incredibly beautiful about the scene. We were safe up there. From the new elevation of the truck bed, we could see beyond the trees and the edge of the hill. All around us was the Mediterranean. It was a brilliant blue and stretched forever until it vanished into the sky. That happens occasionally on Corsica. The mountains block the coastline, so you can forget you're on an island. Then suddenly the water reveals itself quietly, endlessly.

The sun was on its way across the sky, soon to dip behind the western mountain peaks. Everything was turning gold. There was no noise except for the pleasing sound of the goat bells and the wind rattling a couple of hanging pots on the side of the shack. The calm flatness of the water was in striking contrast with the mountains beside us and with the backs and horns of all those goats bumping against each other. The sea was full of possibility and hope. I put my arm around Jackson, wondering if he was taking it in, if he would one day remember that moment and that view.

A loud banging on metal ended the reverie. I looked down and saw two of the more rambunctious hoofed beasts trying to mount the truck. The prospect of being in the confines of the truck bed with Jackson and a couple goats didn't seem good at all. So just as fast as we climbed up, we climbed back down, more awkwardly this time, as I had to maneuver the drop with Jackson in my arms. Before I knew it, there we were, back in the mess of animals.

At this point, I think they knew they had me, could smell my fear. I was visibly agitated, trying to shield

Jackson from the animals that were rearing up on two legs to get a closer look at us. They had driven us up into the truck. And now they had driven us back down from the truck. We were vastly outnumbered, and the goats were only getting more rambunctious the longer we remained among them. I twisted this way and that way, trying to turn my back on the ones that seemed the most aggressive.

I was holding Jackson in my arms, his chest against mine, his back to the goats, but suddenly this no longer seemed high enough and so, desperate to keep him safe, I lifted him up onto my shoulders. I got him up there, but in doing so, I left my midsection unguarded and exposed. The goats saw their opening and wasted no time taking advantage. A frisky kid reared back onto its hind legs and nailed me with a double-hoofed punch straight into my nuts. The pain was immediate and acute. I grunted loudly, folded over and then collapsed onto the ground. Somehow I shielded Jackson from the fall, but he cried in fear and scurried out of my grip.

Upon hearing our yells, Sarah ran from the house followed closely behind by the shepherd. He went right for his animals, stroking a few of their heads and beards and reassuring them with words that sounded half Corsican, half goat. Sarah scooped Jackson up and helped brush me off. We looked at each other. "I was just kicked in the gonads by a goat," I managed to tell her in a weak and labored voice.

It was definitely a low point. I looked awful. Red in the face, surrounded by goat shit, covered in dust, two pathetic empty juice boxes beside me. We burst into laughter. Sarah was full of pity. "You know DB," she said after we had said awkward goodbyes to the shepherd and thanked him for his strange hospitality. "I could never do any of this without you."

"I know," I said, now back in the car trying hard to get us out of that field. "I couldn't either, Sarah." And it was true. I meant it in a big sense—raising our son, finding a path through this world. Still I had just been asked to protect Jackson from a bunch of goats in a shelterless field and had been taken down in the process. I couldn't help thinking that were it not for Sarah dragging us out there in the first place, I would never have had to do any of this without her.

At some point on our drive back to our village, long after I caught my breath, well after I managed to get our car back on a paved road, and after I had stopped feeling sorry for myself, both Sarah and Jackson fell asleep. Looking at Sarah beside me, at Jackson in the rearview, at the mountains we were driving through, I felt a powerful surge of love for them. The "thing with the goats," as I came to call it, left me feeling pretty displaced, pretty far from the world I knew, pretty out of sorts. Still, I had my family. I wasn't alone. Things could never get that bad. I started thinking about what life would be like on Corsica, or anywhere really, without them. The world around me might be just as beautiful, the air just as clean and clear, but all I'd see was their absence.

***

An old man named Antoine lived beside us in our village. He had a little terrace farm on a nearby hillside. He'd be out there at all hours working the land. He particularly liked working in the early mornings. Above Antoine's plot was a flowing spring where we got our drinking water. It came out of a little spout in the mouth of a carved stone lion. We had running water, but the water from la source seemed to taste better. I liked carrying our big glass jug along the moss path, which if you continued on it past a couple of donkeys and broken down huts, brought you to a trail that would lead seemingly forever through the mountains. I would go out there very early in the morning, the moon sitting low in the sky, and if lucky, Jackson still sleeping. There was a stone wall beside the fountain, and I would sit there as the sky lightened.

I couldn't see Antoine from where I sat, but I could hear him working, and when I had my guitar he could hear me. I envied him at work in those early hours. I envied his rootedness. He was born in that village. His mom was born in that village. He knew no other home. I envied what I imagined was his sense of peace and purpose.

In those moments, Antoine and I couldn't have been more different. He seemed almost a part of the landscape. I had moved eight times in ten years, and the closest thing I had to a home was a storage unit in Atlanta that held most of our belongings. There were times, like after that day with the shepherd, or when I was struggling to understand the conversations swirling around me, when I would feel that familiar pit in the stomach, a kind of unease, a restlessness. I was feeling a strange brand of homesickness. The island was so beautiful, how could I long to be anywhere else? What's more, what home was I longing for?

So I imagined a scenario where I was living on Corsica without my family, overwhelmed by a longing for a home that I no longer had. The sentiment was so powerful, a melody came quickly.

As I realized that I didn't have a home to return to, the very concept of home shifted. What I needed was to be with my family, for them to be okay. What I was longing for was them. Home was no longer where I grew up or where Sarah and I had lived together the longest. It was no longer a place in the world at all. It was my family. And if they weren't okay, then I would be unhinged and full of a longing that felt a lot like a longing for home.

(*Play "Homesick" now.*)

HOMESICK

Homesick is hard when you don't know
Just where it is that you call home.

I don't know how this roof's going to hold.
It's oh so cold.
It's been snowing too hard I fear.
Yes I know it's pretty here,
And the air is clear,
But the years aren't passing fast enough this way.
Maybe you can save me now.
I'm not sure how.
I'm calling out for that
I'm crying out for that.

Homesick is hard when you don't know
Just where it is that you call home.

There's a place that the old man knows
Where the moon sits low,
Where he goes to think things through.
I have asked him to think of you.
It may come true.
Been hoping that he might wish you here today.
Or maybe he can lead me home
And not alone.
I'm calling out for that.
I'm calling out for that.

Homesick is hard when you don't know
Just where it is that you call home.
So hold me close, and don't let go,
Cause through it all, I love you so.

Holy riders from days gone by
Come back through time,
Come find me, come quickly, come hear the words I say.
May the world be kind to you
And Jackson, too.
That's all I'm asking for.
That's all I am crying for.
That's all I am praying for.

Homesick is hard.
Homesick is hard.
Homesick is hard.

The shepherd and his goats.

With Jackson in the Restonica Valley, near Corte. (Photo by Sarah Davis.)

A passageway in Tralonca.

This is Tralonca. Our larger apartment, what we called "the grand house," is the one behind and just to the right of the church. (Photo by Philipe Sarthou.)

FATHER - SON
ECONOMICS

"Steel Mill"

We were on Corsica when the American economy started to collapse. Economic ripples spread quickly across the world, and France was hit hard. There was already a healthy anti-American spirit in Tralonca (and throughout France, in fact), but this gave them great new ammunition. As Americans, we were blamed (if half-jokingly) when our neighbors' relatives on the continent were laid off. We were accused of being greedy, wasteful, near-sited, hedonistic. In an unrelated critique, we were accused of being overweight.

Given my lack of language skills, I couldn't really defend myself or my fellow Americans. Still I tried as best I could. I began by looking around at our village. On any given day, weather permitting, the men were tinkering in their gardens. The women were scrubbing their floors, ironing their sheets, making big pots of stew. There was a long leisurely lunch. There was an afternoon nap. When they woke up from those naps, there were games of Boules in the square. Sons paired off with their fathers and competed against their neighbors. Grandchildren ran around the perimeter causing trouble, though never disturbing the games. The women might take a stroll to the neighboring village, gossiping about anything that transpired since their walk the day before. Then many gathered at the village bar or in one house or another for an aperitif before breaking off for long leisurely dinners. It was a beautiful way of life, but it wasn't exactly a viable economic model.

My sample set was of course skewed. Tralonca had a number of older couples living in it. They had paid their dues working for the railroads, the banks, the military. But we made other Corsican friends who did have "jobs"— firemen, bureaucrats, forest rangers. Still, they too seemed always to be in cafes, free to meet up if we needed anything, eager to take off and join in whatever it was we were doing. This was during the winter, spring and fall. In the summer, no one works at all. The French, like most of Europe, take a good month and a half off for their *vacances*.

I mused about how Corsicans had any right to criticize, how they could have anything to complain about, this odd leisure set. I began to understand why the Corsican economy has long been in such shambles, why

Corsica imports so much (even produce from neighboring countries with the same climate and terrain), why Corsicans rely so heavily on French aid. To put it plainly, hardly anyone works a real job. This seemed remarkable to me, and I was initially judgmental, frustrated that they were blaming Americans for anything.

Then I had the secondary and slightly more painful realization: I didn't work a real job either! I fit right in among them. If they were able to take off for a long leisurely lunch and then toss little metal balls around the square all afternoon, well I certainly was as well. In fact I wasn't even taking off from anything. I was just "observing," "thinking," trying to write when inspired. I am exaggerating for I certainly work hard on my music, but I couldn't be fired even if I wanted to be.

In some ways the realization came as a relief. I was not going to lose a job in this downturn. I felt fortunate to be my own boss and, in a sense, to be solely responsible for my fate. But in light of the news coming back from America and other parts of Europe, I also felt guilt. On days when I wasn't creatively productive, when I slipped in among the Corsicans and sipped *pastis* in the early evening, I didn't feel fortunate, I felt selfish.

I haven't worked many conventional jobs. My skill set is quite small, mostly comprising a few things I can do with my imagination. There's not a whole lot I can do with my hands. I can play guitar and type. But I didn't build the guitar I play. I certainly don't know how to repair my computer. I can cook, but I would never be able to catch the food I prepare. I can't tie a very good knot. There's not much in my toolbox. For that matter, there wasn't much in my dad's toolbox when I was growing up. In fact, the only screwdriver I remember seeing in our house when I was little unfolded out of a Swiss Army knife. And I don't recall ever seeing my dad use it.

***

My father taught economics out of graduate school. After a number of years, he left academia to work for his father's company in the garment industry. The business manufactured and imported shirts—t-shirts, button-downs, knits—and then sold them to large retailers. My dad worked together with his dad until my grandfather died, and then my father took over the business.

The office was in the Empire State Building. He took me to work with him when I didn't have school. We rode the train into the city from where we lived in New Jersey. I would hold on tight to his hand as we walked the few long crowded blocks from Penn Station to the big building. I remember having to watch out for swinging briefcases at head level as people in suits rushed and pushed past me. Everyone seemed so important, and my dad was one of them. His office was not many floors off the ground, but it felt like the elevator raced into the sky when the doors closed.

My dad let me help operate the switchboard. "Good morning, Harper Industries," I would say, trying to sound as old as possible, though my voice had yet to change. "How may I direct your call?" I was always worried I would hang up on or misdirect important calls, which I was sure would sink the entire business. There were other jobs as well. I sorted things in the mailroom. Or my dad asked someone to train me on some menial task that involved a calculator. They were creating work for me, but the jobs were always presented as being of vital importance. I took them really seriously.

I worked hard all day, excited by the hustle and pace of it all, and I got really hungry. There was a snack cart that came down the hall around ten o'clock, ringing its bell. On occasion, the person I was working under bought me a pastry or a drink. I loved those days. I was always very excited for lunch, too. My dad would take me to a Chock full o'Nuts or some other noisy lunch counter full of busy people who talked fast about serious things. I was proud of my dad. He seemed to know everything. And he filled with excitement when I asked him questions about the business.

When I was in kindergarten, the teacher asked our class what our fathers did for a living. I apparently announced with great pride that my dad owned the Empire State Building. I had this grand view of him and his importance. Even long after I understood that he didn't in fact own the building, I still felt secure from being able to, in a sense, see him from all over New Jersey and New York. Although his office was only on the 9th floor, he was by extension, all 102 floors and that big radio antenna above.

My dad has scaled back and sold most of the business. There was never any real pressure on me to take it over, though it was made clear that I could if I wanted to in several conversations I remember having when I was much younger and unprepared to think about such stuff. I am not entirely sure if it is a point of pride or disappointment for him that I didn't follow his path. It always felt like he wanted more from me. But to admit that now would mean that he sees limits to his own path, perhaps regrets some of his decisions. Neither he nor I want to think those thoughts.

I don't regret that I didn't choose what he chose. But there is a part of me that regrets not being able to walk in my father's footsteps, to make the commute he made, to have my body move in the way his did, to draw from his experience. As he ages I can't help but think he longs for the same, to still be just as relevant, to be able to teach me all the things he knows and knew, to pass down secrets. I do miss the closeness he describes having with his father as they used to work together. I think my dad misses that closeness, too, as he tries to give me advice about my songs or the music business, tries to understand my life and the particularities of my very different career.

A continuity and symmetry that he had with his father and was mine to maintain has been altered and broken. It's one of the byproducts of growing up in the creative class, in the generation of seekers, of choosers. Without the same level of necessity and with a world of choice, following in the footsteps of our parents seems the last thing we pick. I would never relinquish that freedom to choose. But it does come with a burden, an ironic sort of burden that comes from being free from real burdens.

With all the news coming in from America and other parts of the world of factory closures, I started thinking up a work song. I began imagining the shutting down of a plant where men had worked for generations, men who were specifically trained for that job and little else.

When the protagonist loses his job, he loses everything. It's all he knew. It's all his dad knew. Presumably, it's all his grandfather knew. So he loses more than a job, he loses his whole identity, his whole history. I respect that clear sense of identity. I envy having a real set of skills that you know you're good at. In this sense, a trade is like religion, which draws some of its power because of its history, because the same prayers and songs were sung by sons and fathers all the way back. Losing your job can be like losing your faith.

***

The filial lines seem stronger on Corsica than in America. Even if they were most apparent in our village as fathers showed their sons how to toss Boules balls. Regardless of the lesson, there is greater relevance and

STEEL MILL

There's a steel mill,
Shut down when spring came.
My dad gave his life there,
I was doing the same.

Now I don't know
what to do with my days.
Kingdom comes to workmen,
So the preacher he says.

And there's voices,
Sometimes well you know.
The devil comes a knocking
When the money gets low.

Sing with me please.
Oh da lee, oh da la, oh da lee.
Sing with me please.
Oh da lee.

Yeah it's not like
I liked working there,
The fire and the shovel,
The smoke in my hair.

Oh but lord,
It's all I know.
I miss being needed,
Having somewhere to go.

There's voices,
Sometimes well you know.
The devil comes a knocking
and the bottle gets low.

Sing with me please.
Oh da lee, oh da la, oh da lee.
Sing with me please.
Oh da lee.

Yeah there's a woman
Who gave me the will.
And her name is Gracie.
She believes in my still.

My name is Joseph.
It could well be Job.
I don't mean to harm you
With the hurt that I hold.

Cause it's a story
Heard round each bend.
A man works his heart out
And is broke in the end.

So come on, sing with me please.
Oh da lee, oh da la, oh da lee.
Sing with me please.
Oh da lee.
Sing with me please.
Oh da lee.
Sing with me please.
Oh da lee.

And there's a steel mill,
Shut down when spring came.
I gave my life there.
My dad did the same.

There was a steel mill,
Shut down when spring came
I gave my life there.
Suppose I'd do it again.

(Photo by Sarah Davis.)

II. ELSEWHERE

With Jackson in Fort Greene. (Photo by Alex Weinstein.)

A LOVE LETTER

"The Blood and the Wine"

I grew up on a block full of kids. We roamed and ran through the street and across yards all summer, until well after dark, playing wild games of manhunt and kickball, catching lightning bugs in jars, causing trouble. I remember the feel and smell of the grass, the humid air. If we were playing hide and seek, I remember the fear, waiting and wondering if I'd ever be found. The world was very big, very bright, and I felt all things—good and bad—fully. It's hard to hold on to that. We grow up. We literally grow up. Our eyes and ears and noses get further from the ground. And life gets in the way. We get busy. It takes extraordinary events to reawaken us to those sensations, to the pulse of it all.

Becoming a father was a most extraordinary event. Jackson was born the night before Halloween. Sarah and

93

I arrived at the hospital in Manhattan almost 24 hours earlier. I had practiced every possible driving route from our place in Brooklyn to the Upper West Side hospital. Looking back, some of the routes I tried were completely absurd, but I wanted to be sure, wanted to know all my options, and so I had to weigh potential bridge, tunnel and street traffic at all hours. "If it comes to this," I told Sarah, "I'll run reds. I'll drive up on the sidewalk." But her water broke at one o'clock in the morning, and the roads were basically empty.

In the beginning, labor was slow and relatively mellow. The hospital let us come and go as we pleased. New York is perfect in late October, so we did come and go. We walked in sweaters around Lincoln Center, arm in arm, real slow, stopping every fifty yards or so for her to rest. We went to a little Greek diner. Sarah ordered pancakes. She ate maybe two bites. I had the Lumberjack Breakfast Platter, which I devoured. Then I finished off her pancakes. She was having contractions and so had to get up about every ten minutes and walk around the little tables, leaning over the backs of empty chairs.

This was our first child, and we felt like we sat squarely at the center of the universe. We were aware of contrasting realities. Other people were just starting ordinary days, but for us, it was *the* day. We existed in a magical bubble for most of the morning.

The bubble burst around noon. Delivering without pain medication can be a brutal and almost barbaric thing. I had to support and assure Sarah despite not knowing if it would in fact be okay. I felt like Mickey, Rocky's trainer, unsure of whether or when to throw in the towel. I saw a wildness and fear in her eyes I had never seen before. I also saw a strength and resolve that made me know that whatever challenges would come when our child was in the world, we would be able to meet them. The strength was physical, Sarah literally dragged me to the ground in pain several times. And the strength was spiritual. "I feel like a lion," she told me, after Jackson finally came out and she slowly began recovering. I was in awe and in love with her fully and deeply. It is still hard for me to comprehend that that is the way most of us enter the world.

After that long day finally ended, I realized in a way I hadn't before that I was very glad to be a man. I became awed by women in general. I began to look at new mothers as an odd sort of superhero, armed with a ton of crap, a diaper bag full of all their gadgets and gear, a stroller as their Batmobile.

I felt guilty I couldn't carry the baby for Sarah some of the time, that I couldn't bear some of the pain for her. I also felt an odd kind of jealousy. Our baby was *of* Sarah in a way that he wasn't *of* me. He was literally fed by her blood. The blueprint might have been half mine, but the raw materials were all hers.

Maybe that's why I worked so hard to cook and feed her in the months leading up to the birth. It was my way of trying to give some more of me. If it would be Sarah's blood flowing into Jackson, it was going to be my food that would nourish that blood. I made all sorts of meals: lasagnas and roasts, scones and pies, soups.

I also had a crazy nesting bug. When we moved to New York from Atlanta and had to put half our stuff into storage, Sarah was seven months pregnant. I did basically everything. Although I am terribly disorganized and an incompetent packer—wrapping items that couldn't break even if you tried to break them and neglecting to properly wrap pottery vases or glass jars—I transformed. I created excel files and packing labels. I color-coded boxes by room. Everything was numbered and stacked and sorted. The packing was perfect. It was weird. I was out of control in a controlling sort of way. Even the movers made fun of me, said they hadn't seen such a system before. And after we arrived in our new apartment, I started cleaning. I cleaned rooms and spots I had never cleaned before. Behind the toilet, along the blinds, under the bed, inside the toaster. I dusted cabinets before we unloaded dishes. I wiped out drawers before socks went in. I cleaned doorknobs.

**

When it comes to pregnancy, men and women are really different. Regardless of the level of excitement, commitment and good intention by the expectant father, the relationship between the dad and the growing baby is just theoretical, abstract. I suppose I'm not very good with abstractions. The mother is already building a physical bond. For every moment over the course of nine months, the woman is aware, is preparing. Most men, no matter how modern and desiring, are sort of bumbling around the perimeter, putting their foot in their mouth all the time. We can only try to remind ourselves of the unknown that's coming and try to psyche ourselves up.

Sarah says that before Jackson was born, I rarely wanted to feel him moving around or kicking. Although I sang a lot at her belly, it is true that I felt a little squeamish about the whole idea that there was a little creature growing inside her. Even with our second son, Noah, who was born just after I wrote this book, I was not as excited to feel the kicks as she wanted me to be, as I suppose I should have been. There was something bizarre about feeling that poking and pushing through her belly. I didn't like thinking about the little guy swimming in there in the dark. I didn't know what the kicking meant, if he needed anything, if he was okay.

Though I should have been ready for Jackson's birth, seeing all the changes around me (the growing belly, the crib, all the little clothes, the stuffed animals), I still was totally unprepared when the day arrived. I was utterly amazed and even surprised when Jackson came into the world and was placed in my arms. But then the change was sudden and wonderful, total and terrifying. I was flooded with more love for this brand new, screaming, slightly blue boy with a frightening cone head, than I had ever felt before.

I was stretched in both temporal directions: toward this new future and back toward my parents and my parents' parents. Jackson was born a month after I turned thirty and the day after my father turned sixty. This symmetry felt right. I thought about my dad some thirty years earlier with me in his arms, and my grandfather some sixty years earlier with my dad in his arms. That was some thought. It's only conceptual now, but I felt it with staggering intensity in those first few weeks.

When Sarah eventually came out of the shock of her long labor, she was hungry. I ran outside for food. I was in an altered state myself, electrified and hyper-aware of everything. I remember the elevator ride down from the twelfth floor. "Just had a son," I announced to the fellow riders. I remember the face of the security guard at the front desk of the hospital. I almost hugged him. I wanted to tell everyone.

Many people out that night were in costume, as Halloween was the next day. That felt right. There is a theme that runs through a lot of my music and much of this record, if on a subtle level. It has to do with the relationship between the very personal and the universal. There are times when the two are totally disjointed. Bad things happen to you on a perfectly beautiful day.

At times like these, we can feel very small, very alone. Other times, things feel in synch. The universe seems to amplify or echo your thoughts and moods. There is a god. And that god cares about you. Things feel right and good, even if hard. You feel rooted. The world seems a sympathetic place. With all those people in costume, New York felt that way to me. Everyone seemed aware that this was a special day. Everyone was celebrating, and I was buoyant.

***

Months earlier, Jackson still very much in Sarah's belly, I had been in a period of self-doubt about my ability to write songs and the logic behind my seemingly absurd career choice, which I was stubbornly sticking to. I go through periods like this a lot, and I have more or less learned how to get through them, to ride the waves of insecurity, knowing that they pass. But this one had been going on for months, probably fueled by my fear about what this baby would bring. It was coupled with a lot of rejection and near misses on the business front—tours that fell through at the last minute, TV shows that almost used a song but didn't. I was working on a song I never finished. The first lyric was "I was having quitting thoughts you know." I was trying to write a song about the self-doubt I was dealing with. I was trying to lift myself out of it with a chorus that was positive: "Now it seems there's dreams again, we're dreaming. So much to believe in."

The dream was this baby growing inside Sarah's belly. But to me, it was still only a dream. He wasn't real to me yet. I didn't believe the song and so wasn't able to finish it. The truth was that I really *was* having quitting thoughts. And I wasn't actually having good dreams. The dream of a child, in fact, was doing more to make me want to get a stable job than to write and sing some songs. They say having a baby makes a lot of men change careers, and it almost did for me as well.

Then Jackson came. He changed my heart. Sarah changed my heart. Through it all—the labor, the delivery, the crazy sleep depravity of those early months, the stumbling into parenthood—I fell for both of them in a way I hadn't known would be possible. I felt needed in a way I never had before. Things made sense that hadn't only days earlier. I saw the world again through young eyes. I thought becoming a dad would make me feel old. It did the opposite. I felt like a kid myself. I began taking pictures again, of Jackson of course, but of other things as well. The light on the brownstones in Brooklyn. Leaves blowing from trees. A pattern in the cobblestone.

And I started writing songs again. They were more direct, less esoteric. I worked quicker than I used to. I had to work quicker because naps never lasted long enough and diapers always needed to be changed. My emotions were closer to the surface. Music felt important again. I gave up on that song about quitting thoughts to make room for the new outpouring, including all the songs on *Some Kind of Cure*. But "The Blood and the Wine" came first. It looks backward and forward—back to childhood summers when the world was alive and we were such a part of that world, and forward to having a home someday near a stream, maybe with our children feeling like we felt when we were little. It's a love letter to Sarah. But this new love for Jackson somehow made me able to write it.

(*Play "The Blood and the Wine" now.*)

THE BLOOD AND THE WINE

Tell me that you still remember
When we caught lightning in a jar.

Now you have put the sway back in the grass.
You have put the fire back in me.

There were times when you were hiding,
And I know I've been hard to hold.

But you have put the wine back in the glass.
You have put the blood back in me.

And oh, oh my word.

There's a blue house in the distance.
There's a stream beside it, too.

Well you have put the sails back on the mast.
You have put the breeze back in me.

Oh, oh my word.
Oh, oh my word.
Oh, oh my word.

Now you have put the wine back in the glass.
You have put the blood back in me.

Sarah and Jackson on Dekalb Avenue in Brooklyn.

THE SECOND MOST FAMOUS SQUARE IN THE WORLD

"George Square"

It was early spring, and I was on tour in Scotland sitting in George Square writing a postcard to Jackson. The streetlights were just coming on, and the windows in the buildings that lined the large rectangular space were starting to glow. I noticed a girl crossing toward me at a diagonal. She looked like she was crying.

If you don't know it, George Square is in Glasgow. I've been to that city several times, and when I leave, I always feel a strange pull back. Glasgow is old, Gothic and very beautiful. Many of the stone buildings are streaked with black. It rains a lot, and the water rushes down the sidewalks and hilly streets. The people I've met there are generous, colorful and friendly.

But the city has a different sort of energy at night. I drink more when I'm there. I get heckled more at shows.

I come closer to getting in brawls. There's a feeling that if you're not aware, not at least a little on your guard, something bad might happen, something that might actually involve head butting.

Maybe because of this strange energy, I think I see better when I'm there. It feels like you need to see better to protect yourself, so you do. And there's a lot to see. Tea houses. Museums. The West End. The parks. The university. And there's George Square. Although not necessarily Europe's most picturesque square, I am for some reason always drawn to it, this big open space in the middle of the bustling and sometimes scary city.

So there I was watching the girl as she stopped in front of a few of the statues in the square. She came a little closer and was definitely crying. Not in hysterics, nothing dramatic, but there were tears in her eyes and rolling down her cheeks, and you could see it in the way she carried herself. She got shy when she noticed me watching her. She hid her eyes with her hand. I looked the other way.

I began to wonder what her story was, started imagining a narrative. At first I took her for a tourist, maybe looking to see who the figures were, what they had done. But that didn't seem right. She wasn't looking at the statues the way a tourist or student would. This didn't appear to be the first time she had seen them. I decided that she was turning to the statues for help—the way someone might look at a religious statue. Perhaps something had happened, maybe tragic, maybe existential, maybe just emotional. She was lost and had run out of places to turn for guidance. Of all the improbable places to look, she ended up there, in that public and impersonal square, looking to the stone faces of the Queen, Scottish heroes and famous thinkers for the most private and personal sort of help, looking for some sign of what to do next.

I had been lost like that a handful of years earlier, broken up with my then girlfriend who I had hoped to one day marry. I was living in New York and had recently moved there to be with her. There were days where I literally wandered the streets in any which direction just hoping to bump into something or someone (ideally her) who might get me back on track. New York is a hard city to be lost in. I remember being assaulted by the noise and the speed and the edges of that place. I bumped into a lot of things and a lot of people, none of which helped me in any way. Eventually though, I did bump into the girl I had lost, and we did eventually get married. But that took a long time and a lot of wandering.

***

That evening in George Square was my next to last in Scotland. I had one more show before I would leave for London. A fan who has become a friend had picked me up at the airport when I arrived a few days earlier. He had kindly offered to put me up in his place and to chauffeur me around while I was in the city. He was a chubby-faced man in his mid-thirties with kind eyes and red hair. He looked vaguely like a thinner version of John Candy from *Planes, Trains and Automobiles*. After my plane arrived, we stuffed ourselves and my gear into his compact car and drove off, talking about music and family. He has a child Jackson's age who was born on Sarah's birthday. Small talk. Pleasant, or as pleasant as a conversation can be when you don't really understand a word the other guy is saying.

We drove along a strip of coast with high grass and magnificent views. He gave me a spectacular tour of some of the countryside on our way to the city from Glasgow Prestwick Airport (which I discovered, as we drove on and on, is nowhere near Glasgow). He was proud of his land. I respected this. His roots were deep in Scotland, and his love of it was contagious. There were some enormous houses and a castle or two in the distance.

When we talked our heads were quite close. I tried not to look his way too often, but we happened to turn toward each other at the same time as he stated proudly, "this is where the mountaineers live."

I had spent most of the drive nodding politely. His accent was incredibly strong. I would figure most words out a couple minutes and a few comments later. The conversation was one odd mental exercise for me, as I kept looping back to revise what I thought he had said, what I thought we were talking about. So I kept my part of the dialogue short and vague. But the mountaineer comment didn't make any sense because there wasn't really anything bigger than a rolling hill anywhere in sight. With our foreheads nearly touching, I couldn't hide my confusion. So I asked for clarification.

"Aye. All the mountaineers," he insisted.

"And why is that? Why mountaineers?"

"Not mountaineers!" he said, with a different inflection than mine, "*mountaineers!*"

"That's what I said," I blurted back, feeling trapped now in some bad Abbot and Costello skit.

He said it slower. That didn't help either.

"Spell it for me," I finally insisted, remembering that technically we do speak the same language.

"M-I-L-L-I-O-N-A-I-R-E-S," he said loudly, his face right in mine.

"Ahhh. Shit, Jimmy. I'm sorry." Laughing, I explained what I thought he'd said.

There was awkward silence for a while. Then I hear: "By the way, we're doing some renovations on the house, so you'll be sharing a bed with my wife's mom."

I turned to look at him. Had he really just said that? I asked him to repeat himself. He said it again, far slower and clearer. It was still very difficult to make out his words. "House" had two, maybe three, syllables and a few different pitches, so did "bed" and "wife." "My" sounded more like "me." I wasn't sure what "renovations" sounded like, but I figured that was the only option.

"Sorry?" was all I could muster. I was hoping he had said I'd have to share a bed*room*, not just a bed. But that definitely was not what it sounded like, so I couldn't really be sure. And either way, it wasn't exactly going to be an ideal lodging situation. This is one of the risks (and occasional thrills) of being a musician traveling on a budget. I often have little idea what I'm getting myself into until I'm right in the middle of it. Sometimes it works out. Sometimes it really doesn't. I quickly weighed the cost of a hotel room with the less quantifiable but not irrelevant price of spooning with this guy's mother-in-law, perhaps trying to understand *her* accent all night as we made pillow talk.

"Jimmy," I ultimately asked as politely as possible, "would it trouble you too much to just take me downtown to find a hotel?"

He looked a little crestfallen. But he agreed. "Yeah, sure. It's probably for the best."

After my show that night, he came over to say hello. He liked an older song of mine I played called "Times Square" about a girl lost in all the hustle and noise of that place. He kept saying, "Davey," which incidentally no one else has ever called me, "all this talk of Times Square… what about George Square?"

"What *about* George Square?" I asked him.

"Why not write a song about me and George Square?"

"About you?" I laughed.

"Well at least about the Square. She's really a great old square."

"George is a she?"

Ignoring my question, he went on. "And she's just about as well known as Times Square anyway. She's probably the second most famous square in the world."

That didn't seem right. I was about to rattle off some names of other squares, but I decided to let it go. Turns out, it really isn't right. It's rare more than a couple people at any of my concerts in America have ever heard of George Square, let alone been there.

We had been drinking, and I still felt bad for not staying with him and for all the miscommunication, so I agreed, "sure, sure, James. Give me a few days." I really had no intention of writing the song. Just about every song I've ever written is to some extent about Sarah or now about Jackson. With nothing at all against James, I had a hard time imagining one of the first songs I would write about someone other than my family was going to be about this kind-hearted Glaswegian. And, as fond as I was of Glasgow, I didn't really anticipate setting a song there.

Strangely though, as I was sitting with my guitar a couple days later in the great Central Glasgow Station waiting for my train back to London, the rain pounding down and the pavement outside smelling strongly of spring, a sort of percussive, baritone-sounding guitar part came into my head. The lyric "He was walking cross George Square in the rain" popped out of my mouth.

I laughed out loud. I pictured James, of course, flushed in the face, probably late for something, doing an awkward half walk/half run across the square, maybe struggling with a broken umbrella that kept flipping inside out. I jotted down the chords and the lyric. Then my train came.

Somewhere near the border between Scotland and England, I started thinking about the girl I had seen crying that night in the square. She seemed a more appropriate subject for the song than James. So I changed the lyric from "he" to "she."

What was it that was making her feel so lost? I remembered many times earlier in my relationship with Sarah, when I just wanted to convince her I really did love her as much as I said I did, as I believed I did, times where I just wanted to shake her or shake myself and get us both to realize that our love was the sustaining kind, the enduring kind, that it was something triumphant, strong enough to trump the worries of the world.

Thinking about those memories and looking out on the bleak, wet countryside, I began feeling very lonely. I started to feel sorry for myself, far from home, far from her. The shows on that tour had been hard and not as well attended as I had hoped. The travel was rough. It had rained a lot. England was so expensive, and I wasn't making nearly enough money. I was lugging around too much gear on tubes and trains, in and out of cabs and rental cars. I was tired. I started wishing that train wasn't going back to London at all. I wanted it to take a hard turn, to race across the water, to take me home.

The train of course didn't turn but continued straight

through the heart of England. After a good while (British trains aren't known for their speed), the rain gave way, and the clouds parted a bit. I noticed signs of spring blurring by. Bright grass in the fields. A blush of pink on some little trees. Yellow patches of daffodils. Thick furred sheep on green hills.

Suddenly the sun broke through the clouds, and immediately light poured into the train car. There was this golden glow all around us as we glided on. Miraculously, my whole mood started to change. It somehow gave me new energy. My worries seemed to just break apart like the clouds and disappear. The old country I was cutting through began to look beautiful. The whole world began to look beautiful. I felt awake and alive. I got excited about London, the curry I planned to eat, the show I had that night. And I looked forward to finishing this new song.

I realized something on that train that I've realized maybe a hundred times but it can be hard to hold on to, hard to feel when you're down. Sometimes sadness can vanish, just like that. It's a theme in the song "Parachute" and many of the songs on this record. It actually runs through a lot of my earlier music as well. Knots untie. Clouds pass. Depression lifts. It's not always because you have actively worked through the problem and consciously patched the wound, untied those knots, checked off everything on a list, figured out a solution. It's often less rational and more sudden. It's simpler, if more mysterious. The rain stops. The spring comes.

Maybe you're walking through an open square in some ancient city and you stop feeling so alone. Or maybe you're under a big sky or beside a river and you start to understand your place in time in a new way. Or maybe you're on a train and the light changes. You remember how much you love the person you're with and how much that person loves you. You recall the singularity of your path and your life. You feel lucky to be where you are, who you are, doing what you're doing. You haven't necessarily gotten new answers to your big questions—not from your friends, your family, your god or even some statues. But the questions have shifted, broken up, disappeared. The ghosts are gone. They may come back. But they're gone for now. And that's enough. It's not exactly a solution, but it is "some kind of cure."

(*Play "George Square" now.*)

GEORGE SQUARE

She was walking cross George Square in the rain.
I was high. I was so high in a plane.
I was trying to see through the clouds,
Looking for places we'd been,
like a sign, like a sunburst, like the letters in her name.

Oh girl, don't change your hair for me now.
I am on your side.
No girl, don't hide your hands from me now.
I am on my way down.

She was walking quite slowly all alone.
All the lights in the windows were aglow.
But the statues they were so silent,
With the rain splashing their heads.
How bad she wanted to hear them tell her which way is best.

Oh girl, don't change your dress for me now.
I am on your side.
No girl, don't hide your eyes from me now.
I am on my way down.
I am on my way down.

We were back in George Square when the rain gave way.
There's something in how the spring comes so suddenly.
And the dress she wore was yellow,
And the rain was in her hair.
How bad I wanted to tell her that I would always be there.

So girl, don't change. Don't change. Please don't change.
I am on your side.
No girl, don't hide your heart from me now.
I am on my way down.
I'll be on your side.
I am on your side.

THE MORNING AFTER

"Independence"

In the months before Jackson was born, we were living in a part of Brooklyn known as Clinton Hill. It was what realtors might call "up and coming," right on the edge of the more established Fort Greene neighborhood where we headed for better restaurants, the farmer's market and to see most of our friends. We lived in an old stereo factory that had been converted into white lofts with huge windows and almost eighteen-foot ceilings. I found the place while we were still living in Atlanta and Sarah was pregnant.

Trying to picture our life in the new space was an impossible task. I had no idea what having a baby would be like, what it would require. The place turned out to be perfect, although not necessarily for the reasons I had anticipated. The elevator and ramp up to the building proved to be the most vital features, two perks I had hardly considered. The rest was of secondary value. I had come close to signing a lease on a four-floor walkup. I had no clue just how big Sarah would get and how difficult even one narrow flight of stairs would be. I had no idea how much damn schlepping young parents have to do, how many trips have to be made back up for forgotten things, foreign things, like diaper cream, wipes, burp cloths, pacifiers.

The loft was flooded with morning light. Actually it was flooded with light the entire day. Sarah loves light, so this had swayed me. But I didn't realize how nice it would be for me, up at all hours with Jackson those first few days, weeks, even months of his life staring out our wall of windows over the edge of Brooklyn, watching planes circle around LaGuardia, watching the light come up over the rooftops of Queens.

We lived next to Pratt Institute, which is one of the lesser-known gems of New York. It's an art school, and the campus is a sculpture garden, a little sanctuary. We walked through its grounds hundreds of times, Jackson in a fleece sling against my or Sarah's chest. There were a few new shops were popping up in our neighborhood. Choice was our favorite, a little French café with a brown awning and wooden benches out front. We'd get coffees and read the paper. When Jackson had a few teeth, we would mush up pieces of buttery croissant for him. Or we'd take our drinks and walk through Pratt. We felt young and alive, very lucky and very in love.

We also lived beside the projects. The walk to the subway took us along the edge of towering apartments with small dark windows. The contrast was tough to shake. There is a certain community all new parents share, a level of sleep depravity, wonder and excitement we all experience with brand new babies. Yet mothers coming in and out of those buildings often had a different look in their eyes than we had, a harder look. We were all trying to create warm and safe worlds for our children. Our home was so bright that the amount of light was almost a problem. I would wonder as I'd walk past what it was like in those buildings. I pictured narrow, dark and noisy hallways. When we walked our strollers next to each other, it was hard not to feel the strange hand of fate, brand new babies side by side, living potentially very different realities on the same block at the same instant in time.

We heard gunshots several times near those buildings. One evening in late May, as I was about to round the corner onto my block, a fight broke out in their courtyard. A kid yelled in Spanish, "he's got a gun" and ducked into the corner store for shelter. I ran in after him. From the back of the store where we crouched I could see the crowd of maybe thirty people across the street inside the high-fenced basketball court. There seemed to be two guns, and when one was drawn, there would be an audible gasp, and the children (most of them were just children) would sway and run to the other side of the court. This happened, back and forth for a while. Something in the movement reminded me of the ocean. It was an eerie kind of tide, pulled and pushed by fear of being shot.

Without warning, the boy I had been hiding beside ran out of the store. He had been my guide, staying calm and seeming far more experienced than me in these types of situations. Now that he was gone, I panicked, feeling trapped in the little store with no way out but the front door. I imagined one of the guys with a gun coming in and holding the place up, or the fight just exploding into these cramped little aisles. I would have no chance. So when a bus pulled up between my shop and the basketball court, I decided to run. I sprinted, maybe for the first time in fifteen years, and probably for the first time ever from pure fear. I ran without looking back, down our street, up our ramp and into our building.

The contrast was immense. I unlocked the door to our apartment, sweating and scared, my heart racing. Sarah was feeding Jackson on our big couch. There was music on. Aside from the baby things everywhere, our place was clean, warm and bright. It was early evening, and the sky was glowing.

I struggled to not break down. Relatively speaking, this brush with violence was not a very big deal. But as a new father, I valued my life in a way I never had before. I was depended on. And I was acutely aware of how lucky Jackson was to be where he was at that moment and not around the corner.

***

A couple months later, on the 4th of July, I was really looking forward to watching the fireworks from our loft. Although we had the cheaper view (not toward Manhattan), we did have quite a view of most of Queens and three of New York's less famous bridges: the Triboro, the Whitestone and the Throgs Neck in succession from left to right. We were so sleep-deprived, it seemed staying up until it got dark might actually prove to be a challenge. But if we made it, I was pretty sure we'd get a great show. What I didn't anticipate was just how close and how loud this show was going to be. If there were any displays over the bridges or in the distance over Queens, we couldn't see them.

The projects were aflame. To hell with the puny Roman Candles that had seemed such a big deal when I was little. To hell with fire codes. Some professional grade pyrotechnics were exploding over the tightly packed apartment complex on the corner. Some burst as high and bright as I imagined the fireworks in the city's official display. Some of them didn't shoot color at all. They just ignited with cannon-level noise and strength. We felt them in our stomachs. In our knees. They shook our windows so hard we thought the glass might break. Straight through the night they boomed. Jackson barely slept a wink. So neither did we.

When the aerial attack finally ended and the dawn slowly came, I pulled myself up and took Jackson out in the sling for a drowsy walk and let Sarah try to get some sleep. It couldn't have been much past five. In New York in July, that hour might be the nicest time of the day. The light was just coming into the sky, and it was still cool. But that morning, the air felt strangely thick with ozone and haze from the night before. We walked down to Myrtle Avenue and then cut up across Pratt. As we got to Dekalb, the road and sidewalks were covered with burnt fireworks. Colored wrappers. Charred rockets, spiders, red devils. I walked through piles of ash and broken sticks that looked like spent dynamite. It seemed like there had been a war the night before, and it felt like we had lost.

New York is impressive about street cleaning. The city knows it's just a few bags of abandoned garbage away from being totally overtaken by rats and roaches. Even in this corner of Brooklyn, I was pretty sure all signs of the mess would be gone in a few hours. But Jackson and I got a glimpse of something that it felt we weren't supposed to see. It was how I imagined New Year's Day looks like in Times Square, what a street might look like after a ticker-tape parade.

Because the 4th had just passed, or maybe because I was almost manic from sleep deprivation, my mind was racing. I thought about the morning after revolution, the morning after victory, after independence was declared. I took out my book, rested it on Jackson asleep in his sling and scribbled lines about independence and dreams, about the fear after triumph, about walking the streets in ashes up to our ankles.

I thought about what a bold declaration it had been when America declared its independence. We were just a string of colonies in a wild land with little to no infrastructure, and we broke away from an empire. I doubt we had much of an exit strategy then, just some beautiful ideas. I was thinking about the excitement, the unity, the collective hope as the battles tipped in our favor, as victory seemed imminent. What a shock our leaders must have had when we weren't defeated.

Trudging through the ash on Dekalb, I started imagining the fear that must have followed on the morning after that astonishing victory, something I had never thought about before. What happened when the celebration died down, when sobriety kicked in and when a new nation had to be built? It seemed a lot easier to give speeches and inspire revolution than to figure out what to do after you won, when you got what you said you wanted, when you claimed what you were fighting for. Now to make good on all the promises. Imagine the work. Imagine the scale of it all. A huge mass of land was now momentarily lawless. How quickly did the unity disintegrate? How quickly did factions form once the adrenaline subsided?

***

The Jewish New Year came late that year. It came in October, just a few weeks before Jackson was born. Although I'm not religious, I've always marked Rosh

Hashanah at least in some small way. It's a day of celebration, but what follows are ten serious days. During the "Days of Awe" you're supposed to reflect on mistakes made, things gone wrong. These days lead up to the most solemn day of the year, Yom Kippur. On Yom Kippur you're supposed to fast and apologize to anyone you've wronged over the year, and you're meant to forgive people who have done wrong things to you.

I've always appreciated the pairing of these holidays. Their relationship refuses to allow joy and sorrow, victory and responsibility to disentangle. Though the dates shift, the holidays always happen in autumn, when the summer ends, when kids go back to school, when nights start to get cold. It feels like everything in the world sends the same sort of message at that time, the same reminder or warning: don't be too near-sighted, don't get too carried away, winter is never too far behind summer.

I got Jackson home from our ashy walk while he was still asleep and managed to get him out of the sling and into his crib without waking him. Then I wrote most of the lyrics to "Independence." The song is set on the morning after the victory has been won, as the echoes of the triumphant cries fade, when it becomes clear just how much work there is to begin.

(*Play "Independence" now.*)

INDEPENDENCE

Oh it's the 5th of July,
I was walking the streets.
Everything's over.
Everything's still.

There was still smoke in the sky.
I was holding your hand.
You looked so beautiful.
Your lips start to grin,
Independence.

I think that's singing I hear,
Of heroes and burdens to bear.
I think there's hope now and
light coming through.

Feels like the first of the year.
Eerie, we're all trying to find
Where to start over
And how to begin.
Independence.
Independence.

But all the colors are gone.
Only ashes remain.
They're up to our anklebones.
You pulled me close.

This has been true all along,
We're not free as we feel,
And dreams aren't as simple after we win.
Independence.
Independence.
Independence.
Independence came and went.

Sarah and Jackson in Central Park. (Photo by Gretchen Baudenbacher)

Leaving Fort Greene for Corsica. (Photo by Joel Nettesheim.)

On the London Underground. (Photo by Benjamin Friedland.

Performing at the Bun Shop in Cambridge, England. (Photo by Benjamin Friedland.

Performing at L'oratoire Saint Antoine Abbé in Calvi. (Photo by Sarah Davis.)

Performing at the Freight and Salvage in Berkeley with Jordan Katz. (Photo by Matthew Washburn.)

EMPTY TANK DENIAL

"Parachute"

I believe the perfect tank of gas is one that is totally and entirely empty when you reach the station. If I'm not coasting in to refuel (as I've done more than once), then I don't believe I really need to be there. I'm not necessarily concerned with how many miles I've driven, just that I drove the tank to its full potential. When I'm not in the car, I can think about gas usage with greater clarity. I am not *wasting* gasoline by refueling before my tank is empty. I don't dump the unused gas onto the curb before topping off. I just put less in. Still, when I'm in the car, something takes over. I imagine the leftover fuel festering and solidifying in the bottom of the tank, maybe years old, never to be used. And I don't like it.

I do a lot of driving, and I get an anxious thrill when I push a tank, when I pass the last exit for twelve miles and my car has already been flashing "empty" for a couple of minutes. An illuminated fuel light can focus the mind. On a long drive, this can be enough of a distraction to propel me, to keep me awake. When I make it to the pump, what a relief! What an adrenaline rush! There's a new levity once I've managed to fill up. Now I don't have a care in the world. A burden has been cast off. I feel powerful, reborn, like I could drive forever.

Sarah doesn't wholeheartedly agree with my philosophy. She calls it my "condition." "If you ever go to therapy," she tells me, "I think it's what you should bring up first."

I haven't had a whole lot of automotive trouble. I've only broken down once with a mechanical problem, in fact. It happened to be in Sarah's father's car. But I have run out of gas. Twice, in fact. Neither provided the epiphany that happens when the couple's car in "Parachute" breaks down. But each, in a way, contributed to the writing of the song.

We take so much for granted while driving: the condition of the road ahead, the mechanics of the car, the mechanics of other cars, the dependability and logic of all the other fast moving drivers on the road, the basic continuity of the past into the future. Unless there is an accident, driving confirms our sense there is order in the world, that this order and logic is consistent and sturdy. It lulls us to sleep, psychically, that is. We can't juggle all the variables and all the possibilities. We can't hold onto all of the tiny wonders that driving consists of. So we ignore them and switch to autopilot. But all of a sudden something happens. A car swerves. A pothole appears. A bale of hay falls off the open bed of a truck. The road freezes. Then everything changes. In a heartbeat, all of our preconceptions shatter. Our brains race to rebuild our world. Time halts, as each blade of grass or shard of glass, each bit of pavement, every inch of each car comes into focus and falls back into its place.

A non-responsive gas pedal is perhaps the most innocuous of potential driving calamities. Suddenly you're coasting. There is an abrupt slow down. But a tire hasn't blown. A belt hasn't snapped. You haven't hit the guardrail or been hit by another car. You won't need an expensive repair, just a few dollars of gas. No one is hurt. Your insurance won't go up. You just have to get over to the shoulder. So you hope you're not in a tunnel or on a bridge. You hope it isn't freezing or pouring down rain. You hope you're not in the leftmost lane of an interstate or far from an exit. And you really hope you're not driving with a temperamental trumpet player or worse, a pregnant wife.

***

A few years ago, I convinced Sarah to come with me to a gig in Nashville. It was late spring, and Sarah was four months pregnant with Jackson. She wore sandals and a sun dress and looked beautiful sitting in the passenger seat, her growing round belly poking out between the seat belts. We were coming up from Atlanta, and the fuel indicator went on near the lakes around Chattanooga. There were trucks roaring by on both sides, and Sarah had been nagging me to fill up for a couple of exits.

It was the first time I had really felt it. The gas pedal went down easier than normal. All the way down, in fact. But the car didn't respond. A little bit, maybe. There was a wheeze and a slight push forward. But it definitely did not feel normal. We were in the center lane on I-24. There was barely a shoulder. There were trucks all over the road.

"I think we're out of gas," I said, flat and calm, as if I had little to do with it.

"You've got to be fucking kidding me," Sarah barked back, not the least bit calm.

The steering wheel became pretty tight, but I managed to get us into the right lane and then onto the shoulder, not the easiest thing to do as you're rapidly decelerating and other cars are not.

"Nope. Out of gas. Empty." I tried to sound unconcerned, perhaps even sweet. I made a zero with my finger and thumb, smiled, and then I reached out for her hand, a move that I can now admit was inappropriate.

It's impressive how quickly a coasting car will slow to a stop when there is even the slightest uphill. It shows you how important the gasoline engine really is in propelling a vehicle. I was trying hard to make as little of the situation as possible. "It's fine. It's fine. I'll just run up to the exit," I said with confidence, as we inched to a stop in the car-wide shoulder. "You stay here. Be right back."

Sarah was furious. "You crazy?" she yelled over the roar of the traffic. "I'm not staying here. We're on a fucking highway!" She was right, of course. The shoulder was tiny. I don't know what I was thinking.

Although I could see the exit just a bend up the road, highways were not designed for the common pedestrian. A half-mile can feel really really far when cars are blowing by you at eighty miles per hour and your wife is pregnant and pissed. I kept trying to put my arm around her shoulder, to pull her toward me. Not happening.

I also kept trying to convince her the gas station would be a lot closer if we took the hypotenuse across the field down the embankment to our right. But Sarah didn't like how it looked.

"No way," she said. "We have no idea what's in that field." I wasn't sure what she was afraid of. Snakes? Bodies? But I knew better than to argue, so I held my tongue. We trudged on up the highway toward the exit where we would then jug handle back to the Exxon.

After maybe a minute of walking, a beat up Buick took pity on us and pulled over. "Y'all need some help?" a lady hollered back at us, her head poking out from the passenger-side window. Her southern drawl was basically unintelligible, not a whole lot easier to understand than my Scottish friend's accent.

"He ran out of gas," Sarah shouted back, waving her thumb in my direction. It was true. It was my fault not ours collectively. Still the third person pronoun stung a little.

"Y'all hop in. We're getting off anyway," the lady yelled.

We squeezed in beside two extremely large children of undeterminable ages. I remember accents so southern and strong that there was little point trying to talk. Yet, I also remember that Sarah, who isn't normally very talkative among strangers, couldn't wait to chat it up with them, as if after driving for two hours with me, she finally felt she was among people she could relate to.

"This wasn't his first time, you know," Sarah announced immediately as I closed the door. "He's always almost running out of gas!"

The entire few minute drive involved them collectively ridiculing me and suggesting that Sarah would be better off making her way alone in the world or staying and raising our baby with them. Luckily she didn't agree to either proposition, and we both got out of the backseat at the Exxon, thanking them warmly. I bought a Gerry can, put in a gallon or so, and we began our trek back to the car.

This time, the temptation to cut across the Wendy's parking lot and out across that field was too strong, even for Sarah. We set off. It seemed like a good idea for the first five minutes or so. The grass was long, and there was a strange and unique, post-industrial American beauty to the scene. We were in the Cumberland Plateau, and a stretch of the Appalachians rose around us. The colors felt supercharged. The sky was bright blue. The clouds were a brilliant white. The big and perfectly straight strip of silvery interstate whizzed by. The shiny signs seemed to glow. And there we were—holding hands now, as Sarah had finally begun to soften, smile a little and let me back in—walking across this oddly empty expanse of unused grassland, a vintage leather handbag in her other hand, a red plastic jug of fuel in mine.

This postmodern calm ended when the field started to get a bit wet. "Marshy" is a word one might use. The marsh quickly turned to bog, and the bog became more or less like a sunken swamp. Sarah, you might remember, was in sandals. At first we figured it was just going to be a couple of puddles, a wet patch. You figure something like that will dry up. So we forged ahead. But then, before we knew it, we were in deep enough that it was really unpleasant. We were too far in to turn back. Needless to say, Sarah dropped my hand. She slogged on ahead.

Who knew what we were walking through? Up until that moment in Sarah's pregnancy, I had been worried about anything and everything she breathed, anything she put in her mouth, anything that touched her skin or went in her hair. Now I had led her into the runoff from a major interstate, a few fast food restaurants, a couple of gas stations and lord knows what other kinds of crap.

When we came to the base of a hill, above which was the highway and our waiting car, the land began to dry out. "Thank god," I shouted up at Sarah.

She didn't respond or even look back. She was waiting for me, arms at the hips, looking off toward the hill and sort of shaking her head. "There's a frickin' fence here," she screamed.

It was low enough to scale. But there was this small strip of barbed wire curling on top of it. It was just barely barbed. But it was barbed.

"Should we go back?" I asked nervously.

She said, "hell no" and without hesitation chucked her sandals and bag onto the other side. Then up and over. Man, I was in love with her. It took me quite a bit more maneuvering, but we both made it without scratches or cuts. There was a cop about to ticket our seemingly abandoned car when we appeared. He agreed to let us go with just a couple disparaging remarks in my direction after he took one look at Sarah's belly, the mud on her legs, the look in her eyes.

We put enough gas in to get us back to the Exxon, and then we filled up the proper way. We washed all the muck off our legs in the restroom and drove the rest of the way to Nashville in silence.

***

A couple years went by without incident. Jackson was born. We moved to New York and then to Corsica. Upon return to America, we purchased a used fuel-efficient hybrid vehicle. A Prius. It has a computer screen that tells your average mileage per gallon and also gauges what your getting at the moment. You can watch the bar drop as you rev the engine and see it soar to a hundred miles per gallon when you coast down a hill. For the first few months driving the car, I was obsessed with that screen. It changed the way I drove. I no longer hurried anywhere. I drove a lot slower. I took my foot off the gas, using gravity whenever possible. I looked condescendingly on drivers who honked and cut me off. I certainly looked condescendingly at drivers of big SUVs. I wasn't necessarily a safer driver, just a slower, more self-righteous one. My habits pissed everybody off who drove with me. "It feels like we're in a golf cart," Jordan (my trumpet player) would say. I'd ignore him, going on and on about my mileage while we rolled comfortably and quietly toward whatever gig we were heading to.

My driving eventually returned to normal. And as it did, I found that my empty tank denial was still strong. In fact, it was perhaps stronger. In the Prius, it seemed literally impossible to run out of gas. I got almost fifty miles to the gallon on good days. The computer told me everything. I could estimate how much gas I had left with near pinpoint accuracy.

Because of this technology, when Jordan and I were en route to a show in Memphis, I knew we could make it another ten miles to refuel at the exit that had a Panera. I ignored his advice at each of the prior three exits to get gas. I don't regret waiting until the Panera exit. What I do regret, however, was that I didn't pull right into the gas station when we got off. I insisted we eat first.

When we got back into the car and I pressed the ignition button, a red triangle with an exclamation point lit up. I hadn't seen that one before, so I just ignored it and pulled back out toward the gas station. We made it maybe thirty feet down the road, and then the gas pedal had that familiar lightness. I knew the feeling. You don't forget it.

I turned to Jordan. "Empty," I said, as nonchalantly as possible.

The look Jordan gave me was different than Sarah's had been when I told her we ran out of gas. There was still some love behind Sarah's glare, if buried deep. Maybe it said, "I can't believe I married you." But it still said somewhere, "this is the man I married."

Jordan's was simpler. Something like, "you are a stupid, stupid man." The act seemed to trump three years of touring together, seemed to negate any impression made by our years of friendship and touring together. He just shook his head and decided that my brain was pea-size, my skill set non-existent. As I set off on foot across the I-20 overpass to purchase three bucks of gas and yet another red jug, I had to admit he was kind of right.

***

I never thought about it until then, but standing at a gas pump without a car beside you is an inherently shameful experience. It's like walking up to a takeout window at a Taco Bell. People look at you funny. You feel the need to explain, to qualify.

Somehow I didn't learn this lesson the first time, but if you are filling a Gerry can with gas, you should do at least one of two things, and you might as well do both: 1) Don't pull back fully on the pump throttle. 2) Be sure the spout of the jug is pointing away from you.

Well, I did neither. So the gas charged into the can, and then immediately the gas charged right back out of the can. It exploded out the spout and sprayed me squarely and strongly in the face.

The sting was instant and impressive. I screamed. Thought I had been blinded. Gerry can still in hand, gasoline dripping off my face, my first instinct was to grope blindly for the eye wash station—that squirt bottle by the door in every high school chemistry lab. Then I thought about dumping the dirty bucket of windshield washer water over my burning head. Luckily I resisted that temptation. Instead, I dropped the can and, with eyes squinted shut, barely able to see at all, I staggered into the station.

"Bathroom," I muttered as I got inside. Then I hollered it again. "Bathroom!" Someone quickly grabbed me by the arm and led me to a sink, no questions asked. Had this happened enough times that the BP had established protocol? The faucet was turned on for me, and then I was left alone. I splashed water onto my face for maybe five solid minutes, cursing and moaning until most of the sting was out and I could cautiously open my tightly closed eyes. Blurry light came in. Not blind. Thank god.

I gathered myself together, my face feeling really strange, my clothes absolutely soaked and retrieved the can I had dropped. Somewhat nauseous from the fumes and the heat, I again tried to get a gallon of gas, this time pulling up ever so gingerly on the handle, holding the container at arm's length and pointing the spout far away from my face. I still flinched as the gas went in. Then I walked back to the car to find Jordan leaning on the hood calling all the people in my life whose numbers he had: Sarah first (who wasn't at all surprised), then my manager, my agent, mutual friends. He was suggesting that they all reevaluate their opinions of me and stop trusting me with anything important.

I began filling the tank. SUVs and truck drivers honked and laughed. One guy flipped me off. Jordan just grinned at me and shook his head. My eyes were puffy. My cheeks were tingling. My clothes were wrecked. And we were now going to miss our sound check. As I stripped off my shirt and considered throwing it out the window, Jordan sparked up a bowl and nearly lit my body and our whole vehicle on fire. It would almost have been fitting.

***

For the most part, I learned my lesson, if a little late. I haven't run out of gas since. But I'm still obsessed with what can happen when there is an unforeseen break in the norm and we are thrust suddenly out of the ordinary. There's a part of me that wants to be lying on the hood of that broken down car under the autumn sky in "Parachute." Certainly I would rather be on that hood than trying to wash gasoline out of my eyes or explain to my pregnant wife why we need to take a little walk along the interstate.

It's one reason I like songwriting—you can change a detail or two and create something romantic out of something that might just be a really big pain in the ass. But I don't think that sort of romance is only possible in fiction. And maybe that's why I still don't see the refuel indicator in as urgent a light as I should. I can't seem to quite kick the curiosity of the unknown, wondering if we'll make it to the next exit and, if we don't, what will await us on the side of the road.

(Play "Parachute" now.)

PARACHUTE

Your heart is like a parachute.
It only opens when you fall.
Ba ba ba ba ba ba ba ba ba…

Driving back to Massachusetts in your father's car,
Top down, we saw all the stars.
I've been waiting for the fall to get back where you are,
Top down and talk about it all.
Top down. Top down.

Your heart is like a parachute.
It only opens when you fall.

Driving back to Massachusetts in your daddy's car,
Broke down. Yeah, we broke down.
Lying back against the windshield, cars were blowing by.
And you cried, wrapped up in my arms.
You cried. You cried.

Your heart is like a parachute.
It only opens when you fall.
Your heart is like a parachute.
It opens when you're falling down.
But look at me, I'm falling now.
Come let me pull you open.

And oh, you and I, autumn sky, trying to see so far.
Oh, autumn sky, you and I, trying to see too far.
Ba ba ba ba ba ba ba…

Driving back to Massachusetts.
I believe, this is who we are.
I believe. Oh, I believe.

Your heart is like a parachute.
It keeps us both from falling down.
Your heart is like a parachute.
It keeps us both from falling now.
Ba ba ba ba ba ba ba ba…

(Photo by Matthew Washburn.)

III. CORSICA 2

Tralonca in early spring.

SINGING WITH
THE CORSICANS

"Shenandoah"

The first time I sang with the Corsicans, it felt more like wrestling than making music. It was after one of the many mountain pilgrimages Sarah dragged us on. I was grabbed over the shoulder by Pierre Paul and pulled in close. Corsican men typically sing in tight clusters known as *equipes*, or teams. And the experience felt like that. Like I was in a huddle. Intense. There were four of us in this circle. We sang with (or at) each other at staggering volumes for the next half hour or so. It was electrifying. And it was a little scary.

The other men were wearing fatigues. There was kindness in their eyes, but there was also some violence. Each carried a knife. No one used his knife, but each had one. If you had to compete with these guys, you definitely wanted them on your side. I was pretty sure they could kill a man if need be. I was pretty sure at least one of them had.

I had watched and listened to this Corsican singing our whole year with fascination and anxiousness, both wanting and not wanting to join in. I heard it most on these pilgrimages, sacred rituals where people would ascend to the ruins of some ancient chapel and observe a mass. After the mass ended, the men gathered under chestnut trees, passed bottles of pastis and sang their lungs out for the rest of the afternoon.

We went on these pilgrimages for Sarah's work. She recorded their songs and ceremonies and conducted interviews. The hikes were always a lot harder than we were told they'd be, and the rituals lasted a lot longer than we expected they would last, but without exception they were the most memorable adventures of our year. I was always amazed by how many people went, young and old, in good weather and bad, particularly considering how strenuous some of the hikes were—to abandoned villages miles into the mountains, to shrines on peaks that at times required scrambling on all fours. The mass itself always seemed the least important part of the day, although everyone was respectful. A handful of men would listen and participate, but most stayed on the perimeter and waited for the service to end. The important part was really the eating, the drinking, the fellowship and, of course, the singing that followed.

After the mass, a few men would fire off rifles. Then we'd descend maybe half the way back down the mountain to where we had left our food and alcohol. The picnic spots were always well chosen, often beside a stream, always in a grove of shade-providing chestnut trees. We would spend the rest of the day feasting and listening to men sing.

Women would break out trays of smoked meat and wedges of melon. Baguettes were passed. Wine and pastis that had been cooling in the stream were opened. Fires were lit. They roasted chestnuts and seared blood sausages over coals piled on the ground. The food was always strong and good. Rich and extremely salty. Everyone had impressive knives. Even the women. The gatherings were convivial and boisterous. And they always went on way too long. People got very drunk. Once the men started singing, they never wanted to stop.

On our first pilgrimage we hadn't been told that we should bring lunch and so had only snacks for Jackson. Everyone else had bags and baskets full of things to eat and huge extended families to share it all with. Without any close friends, we felt out of place to begin with, the only foreigners present for this very local tradition, but we felt particularly uncomfortable watching others eat. To our amazement, we were quickly embraced and offered one thing after another by nearly all who were there. It took us a full year to earn that kind of acceptance in our village.

Most of the songs sung are in the traditional form known as the *paghjella*, which is basically a three-part chant that begins with the baritone melody, followed by a bass entrance and then a high tenor accompaniment. The harmonies are Western, but the style of singing feels less so, more Arabic, more medieval, perhaps. Voices waiver. Pitches bend. And harmonies become minor only to lift and resolve somewhat unexpectedly. The singing is very loud. The performances are rough, imperfect. Sometimes they are stunning, in the way something wild is stunning, like a vast desert or a raging thunderstorm. The songs capture something hard about Corsica, something tragic and sad but ultimately very beautiful.

That's when the songs are at their best. But they aren't always at their best. Sometimes they can actually be very hard to listen to. On a couple occasions, I thought it was almost a joke—how loud and out of tune the men were singing. I had a hard time keeping a straight face. But the singers and everyone listening were deadly serious, even emotional.

The singers are generally tense, neck muscles and veins bulging. Their faces go red. Their eyes go wild. There is nothing dainty about it. Possibly excluding Tuvan throat singing and a Georgian choir (who perform with swords hanging off their robes), it is the most manly singing I have heard. The music isn't performative. The goal isn't the same as it is here. I never totally shook the critic in me, but he did grow quieter as I got lost in the experience and the setting of those songs.

Once the pastis was opened, an impromptu competition of sorts would break out. One group would start singing. When they finished, another would start up quickly. Then another would begin. After a while the groups might not even wait until the earlier trio had finished. The battle was won by volume and endurance. The friends who brought us on most of these pilgrimages were almost always the last and the loudest singing.

Because our hosts would sing until the end, it was really hard to ever leave early. Jackson often was way past his breaking point. I was often way past my breaking point. Sarah, however, was in her element, mesmerized by the songs and the commentary, soaking up the setting and the camaraderie.

***

After this one particularly long hike and picnic, I was amazed when Pierre Paul, who had been singing at peak volume all day, wanted to sing some more. His equipe was heading back to his house, and he told us that we absolutely had to come. Non-negotiable. Honestly, it was the last thing we wanted to do. Our day had started before dawn, as it had been a long and treacherous drive to get to where the pilgrimage began.

Being a good and grateful Corsican guest, however, means always submitting, never saying no. Invitations were not offered just to be polite, as is often the case in America. If asked, we were obliged to say yes. So, like on many other occasions, we consented, dragging Jackson on to yet another round, attempting to follow Pierre Paul's car as he rocketed around the white-knuckle curves and down the mountain to his house.

It was there that I was abducted, pulled from my pleasant conversation with Sarah and the other women, pulled away from Jackson and the other children, pulled into the kitchen. And there, beside an enormous simmering stew, we began to sing. I had never been asked to join before, but now in private, our hosts were eager to sing with me.

I didn't know the songs, so I sang bass, which was easier to manage, easier to fake. I don't have a particularly low voice, and I rarely sing loudly. But testosterone (and steam) was everywhere, and I sang lower and louder than I had thought possible. It was a strange feeling. I felt like I was both with and against them. We sang at each other in a way that was meant to provoke and push. Yet we also sang together, ultimately supporting and blending.

Usually when I sing with other people, I try to lose myself in the other voices or allow other voices to get lost in mine. We aim to get our notes to vibrate at the same pace, so that all separation disappears. Not so here. This was more of a show of strength, an act of survival. They were insisting that my voice bend toward theirs. I was doing the same. Yet ultimately, somehow, it all resolved, somehow we all came out victorious.

During and afterward, we drank. We laughed. We slapped each other hard on the shoulders and backs. A bond was built through the singing that endured for the rest of the evening and the rest of the year whenever I saw those men. It was a bond I imagine might be shared by men who hunt together or hold some secret about a crime they once witnessed or, perhaps, committed.

Scenes like this happened several times over our year, though the great majority of the time I would just listen to others sing. After long dinners or at parties with the right mix of people, though, I might sing with a few of the men. Mostly it strengthened our bonds. Occasionally I'd feel something about another person in a circle that made me afraid and not want to be near him again. It was like a form of dating. Some dates went well. Some really didn't.

***

Relatively early in our year, an article came out in the local Corsican paper about Sarah's work. It mentioned she was living on the island with her son and her husband, and that I was an American singer. After that, it became quite easy for me to book concerts. And I did ultimately perform a lot of concerts. Some were in ancient town squares, some in very old churches, some on beaches accessible only by boat. Each was unique and memorable.

The treatment by the promoter was always first rate. It was assumed I would dine with whomever booked the show. That meant I would be taken to a long dinner at a restaurant or that the host family would prepare me a massive, home-cooked meal of Corsican fare, often featuring a rich boar stew, astonishingly powerful cheese and endless amounts of wine. The meals, which seemed more important to the promoters than the concerts themselves, included a lot of extended family at a long table.

I was always invited to stay the night. It was rude to say no. Maybe the grandmother would be asked to sleep elsewhere, and they insisted I take her bed. Or a child would sleep on the couch so I could have his room. These nights were always at least a little awkward, as language was still a major issue. Their kindness was consistently over the top, and I never could express sufficient gratitude or gracefully decline their gifts and excessive hospitality.

The concerts were primarily memorable for me, though, because I spoke (or tried to speak) only in French between songs. Given my level of proficiency, this was a relatively absurd endeavor. Although my French definitely improved as the year went on, I was never even close to comfortable talking, and I certainly couldn't think on my feet and make up stories the way I liked to in English. That didn't mean I didn't try. I would often start on some topic or line of reasoning to introduce a song that I couldn't get out of. My tangents would trail off or just end abruptly as I realized I didn't have anywhere near enough vocabulary to go on. There were a lot of long, awkward pauses. There was a lot of utter nonsense. And there was an awful lot of repetition, as all I could do is try a different combination or new sequence of the few handfuls of words I knew.

I primarily played my own songs at concerts. But traditional music was such a big deal on the island, such a point of deserved pride, that I wanted to mix in traditional American songs when I performed. The Corsican music so captured the rough beauty of the landscape and culture, and I wanted to share something similar from America that might balance out the mindless American pop music that had infiltrated even the most remote villages. I also wanted to find a song that in its own way countered all the negativity toward Americans, an American song that felt and sounded like the America I believed in, that captured my feelings for my country—feelings that were surprisingly growing stronger and deeper the longer we were abroad. Sarah reminded me of the song "Shenandoah." I remembered I had sung it in eighth grade chorus, before my voice had changed. The melody was still with me, and I remembered most of the words.

I would introduce "Shenandoah" as an American song, a song of my homeland. I introduced the song the way Corsicans might introduce one of their more popular traditional songs, like it was sacred. I would try in badly butchered French to convey the openness in the song, its vastness.

The sense is that the singer has been away, maybe at war, still in America most likely, but far away from home. That possibility—of being within America and yet worlds away from your home in America—is something very hard for many people in other parts of the world to grasp. The sheer size of our country wasn't comprehensible to most of the Corsicans. Our micro-cultures and microclimates, our different colors and fabrics, the foreignness on our very soil, we can be so many different things and still be American. This is not true at all on Corsica.

When I sang "Shenandoah," I could feel regards soften, feel audiences come to like me, to like us. Even if they didn't understand the words, I believe they felt the expansiveness and, somehow, the humbleness of the song. I believe they felt the openness of the melody. I love that about music. That you can feel the power of the song even without getting the words, that you can come to love the singer without understanding anything he says.

"Shenandoah" is perfect for this. There is something so pure and simple about the melody. It feels like a part of nature, like it has always existed. It sings of a very basic longing and love for where you're from. That can be felt in every note. It's a universal sentiment, and I was glad to let people know that my family and I, that Americans in general, were part of that same universe.

In the end, "Shenandoah" is also an individualist's song. Even if it's a song of longing, it's a song sung by a traveler, a wanderer. He hasn't been home in seven long years, but he's bound to leave again by the end of the song. It's the song of a pioneer, an explorer, a seeker. That message spoke to me then. It speaks to me now. And it certainly gets to the heart of the American spirit.

So when it came time to record my album, although I rarely put covers on my records, I wanted to include "Shenandoah." It was important to us every time I sang it. And I sang it throughout that year, not in the tight circle of Corsican singers, but alone. Not from the top of a mountain, but from wherever I stood. Not loudly, but with an equally full heart.

(*Play "Shenandoah" now.*)

SHENANDOAH

Oh Shenandoah, I long to hear you.
Away you rolling river.
Oh Shenandoah, I long to hear you.
Away, I'm going away,
Cross the wide Missouri.

'Tis seven long years since I last saw you.
Away you rolling river.
'Tis seven long years since I last saw you.
Away, I'm going away,
Cross the wide Missouri.

Oh Shenandoah, I love your daughter.
Away, you rolling river.
Oh Shenandoah, I love your daughter.
Away, I'm going away,
Cross the wide Missouri.

Oh Shenandoah, I long to hear you.
Away you rolling river.
Oh Shenandoah, I long to hear you.
Away, I'm going away,
Cross the wide Missouri.

Oh Shenandoah, I'll never leave you.
Away you rolling river.
Oh Shenandoah, don't want to leave you.
Away, I'm going away,
Cross the wide Missouri.

Pilgrimage to chapel above Sermano. (Photo by Sarah Davis.)

DEATH IN THE VILLAGE

"Marie"

In August, a woman in our village died. We had never met her. She was sick and housebound when we arrived, and she was transferred to a hospital shortly thereafter. We learned the news early one morning when a neighbor knocked on our door and told us in a hushed voice. She was only 44 when she died, and her daughter had given birth to a baby girl only days earlier. Outlived by two generations, younger and older, the woman left behind a mother, a grandmother, a daughter and now a granddaughter all of whom still lived in Tralonca. She had a husband too, a silver-haired cattle owner who didn't talk or smile a lot.

Though not as precariously perched as some of the Corsican hilltop hamlets, Tralonca is still far from being on flat ground. Its physical position is a metaphor of sorts for its lack of stability and durability. While

Tralonca can trace its existence back over a thousand years (and most of the families there can trace their lineage that far as well), in many ways life there feels very fragile. The village, it sometimes seems, is fighting hard to hang on and survive. Certain people are like the pillars of the place. If they die or move away, I'm not sure the community will hold. As the old far outnumber the young, it's hard to imagine how the community will survive even if everyone there remains.

We came to see the precarious positioning of Tralonca as a sort of glue. People need each other. It is not the same village of old—before the road came, when they had to produce their own food, educate their own children, entertain themselves, and where leaving meant a long and rough donkey ride. But there is still great mutual social dependence among villagers. The elders are revered. The young are the hope for the future. Every person brings a skill to the collective.

It's of course a tragedy when anyone dies young. And it's a tragedy when anyone dies in a village of only forty people. But when someone dies young in such a small village, it's a double tragedy.

Virtually everyone in a Corsican village is also somehow related, if not directly then through marriage. Everyone seems to be at least a distant cousin. So when this woman passed, it seemed as if the entire town lost a member of its family. The fragility of our little village made that loss all the harder to bear.

**

August is a time of great festivity on Corsica. There are performances, concerts and parties nightly. Most villages host their big annual *fêtes*. It is absurd, really. Practically nothing goes on for months on the island, and then summer rolls around, and you have to choose between festivals and a number of family gatherings. We were double and triple booked on most nights during July and August, requiring some tactful social navigation so as not to offend.

The day we found out about the death, a big beverage truck had just delivered hundreds of cases of beer and champagne for our village's annual party that was supposed to happen only a few days later. All the kids (and nearly all the grownups) had been talking about this party for months. It was cancelled immediately when the news came. All the cases of drinks remained stacked, a sad and enormous pile in our little town square waiting to be picked back up by the same truck that dropped them off.

We happened to see that truck when it pulled up to unload. It was huge by Corsican standards and getting up our little road was no small feat. Turning around in the town square took him nearly half an hour.

The only way in or out of our village is the winding, one-lane road that wraps around smaller hills for several miles of hard turns. Depending on the direction of the switchback, the driver or the passenger is often hanging over the edge, and there is no wall or fence or any retainer to shield you. Apart from a few places, there are no shoulders either. Should another car be coming (particularly around one of the countless blind turns), there is very little you can do. Pull to the right and you go over the edge. Pull to the left and you slam into the rocky hillside. Continue on and you crash into the oncoming car. So you jam on your brakes, making eye contact with whomever is coming— and you most certainly know the driver, perhaps it's the lady who delivers bread every morning, perhaps it's your next-door neighbor. Maybe she glares at you a minute if she thinks you were driving recklessly or doesn't like you. Then one of you, and it was almost always me, backs up around a bend or two, until the road is wide enough for the other car to pass.

Up until very recently, there was no line painted on the road. Now there's a white dotted line up the middle, a humorous suggestion that it is a two-lane road. The real value of the paint was that at night we just straddled it with our left and right tires, knowing that so long as we had a tire on each side, we weren't going to drive off the edge.

We ultimately decided it was safer to drive the road at night, despite the fact the edge was impossible to see. We could see headlights of oncoming cars from way off and so had ample time to find a relatively wide straightaway and wait. More significantly, we couldn't see how long our fall would be if we were to careen over the dark cliff, something we preferred not thinking about.

**

On the day of the funeral, it was basically impossible to drive on that road. There were cars parked along both sides for more than half of its five-kilometer length going up to our village and for at least a kilometer past our village. This was our first Corsican funeral. We had heard that funeral rituals were a really big deal on the island, but we had no idea. Apparently, if anyone in your family knew anyone in the family of the deceased, someone in your family had to attend. People read the obituaries in the local paper more religiously than any other section. With the degree of separation on an island like Corsica about three, or maybe even two, Corsicans go to a lot of funerals.

Nearly one thousand people packed into the little church and spilled out into the village square. Some sat on the cases of beer and champagne. Most didn't wear black. Many wore white open shirts, linen pants, sunglasses. People leaned against the walls and stood on the steps. They spread up the hillside. The vast majority didn't enter the church or try to hear the priest. But they were there. And they made sure that the family of the woman who died knew they were there.

The bells rang that morning for what seemed like hours. We dressed Jackson up and held his hand tightly.

We made our way into the church and paid our respects, mumbling our condolences awkwardly and respectfully. We kissed the family and close friends and tried to do the right thing. Then we tried to stay out of the way, retreating to the edge of the square. We watched.

We saw the daughter and newborn granddaughter of the deceased. We saw her mother and grandmother. They were shaking with grief. We saw children, normally so loud and rambunctious, now grave and looking so grown up. We saw the whole family and all the inner circle of our village distraught.

And we saw Marie, an adorably shy six-year-old girl whose grandparents lived in a house just beneath ours. Marie didn't understand much of what was going on, but she was quiet and respectful, clinging hard to her mother who was weeping. Her mother kept reaching down to brush Marie's hair out of her eyes, tucking strands behind her ears.

I had a soft spot for many of the children in our village. But I was particularly fond of Marie. She had big cheeks and brown hair cut in bangs. Constantly riding her bike too fast down cobblestone hills, trying to catch up to or play with the older boys, she was always getting bruises and hurt feelings. We would notice her curiously and quietly watching us as we hung our laundry or sat down earlier than the rest of the village to eat dinner, as I played guitar on the terrace. Appearing on the edge of the scene, she would peek around the corner of our stone house or stand just below our terrace looking up. With my level of French on par with, say, a bashful kindergartener, I came to see her as a sort of equal. She represented some kind of ideal of innocence—old enough to understand but not yet opinionated or jaded.

***

The funeral was the first time I realized it, but the people in our village almost never showed weakness. They weren't always friendly, by no means were they always friendly, but they almost always appeared strong. They very rarely fought in public or let any familial disputes escape their closed shutters or thick walls. And they never displayed sadness. Maybe this was cultural. Or maybe it was out of necessity—knowing that strength was needed to hold each other and Tralonca up.

For the first time in our year, grief was everywhere. We didn't expect to be moved. We hadn't really been accepted yet by most of our neighbors. It was happening, but it hadn't happened yet. There were still a number of them who didn't like that we were even in the village at all. Despite this, and despite the fact we didn't know the woman who died, hadn't talked much to her husband or daughter, Sarah and I were a mess. Without warning, I broke down. I felt death in a way I hadn't since my grandfather had passed away more than fifteen years earlier. It was palpable and frightening.

I couldn't contain my sadness or hide it from Jackson, who didn't understand anything that was going on, certainly not why his dad was crying. I broke down for him first, thinking about Jackson losing one of us, thinking about all the people he would lose through his life. I also broke down for my parents, thinking about them getting older and dying. I cried because we were so far away from comfort, from home, from most of the people we knew and loved.

More surprisingly, though, I grieved for the kids of our village. I grieved for Marie. I felt the tragedy most through her eyes and the eyes of the children of Tralonca. I mourned for Tralonca, this magical and vulnerable world that seemed to be crumbling around us. And in my mourning, it began to feel for the first time like *our* village.

(*Play "Marie" now.*)

MARIE

A wounded town, where the winds won't blow,
The rain won't fall, but the clouds won't go.
Well there's a fallen man hears a minor tune.
There's an empty bed, and there's an empty room.

With the shudders closed and the fire low,
The rains won't fall, but the stars won't glow.
Well there's a lonely girl, and her dress is torn.
A baby knows when her mother mourns.

Oh Marie, it's not like me to fall apart.
Oh Marie, it's not like me.

A wounded town and the hill below,
Rains won't fall, but the winds won't blow.
Cause when a village turns into walls and woes,
And a father's hands can't patch the holes.

Oh Marie, it's not like me to fall apart.
Oh Marie, it's not like me.

The old church roof, caved in long ago.
But its bell still rings, so sad and slow.
Cause when a body burns into smoke and soul,
And a father's hands can't patch these holes.
No a father's hands, can't patch these holes.

Oh Marie, it's not like me to fall apart.
Oh Marie, it's not like me.
Oh Marie, it's not like me to fall apart.
Oh Marie, it's not like,
Oh Marie, it's not like,
Oh Marie, it's not like me.

The Corte Citadel

Sarah in the Tavignano Valley, near Corte.

The Girolatas, one of the more spectacular spots I performed
The concert was in a large tent on a beach accessible only by boat or a full-day hike

Cappo Rosso, near Piano

(Photo by Sarah Davis.)

THE THINGS
THEY CARRIED

"Soldier's Song"

Graveyards are all over Corsica. They are full of raised mausoleums like the cemeteries in and around New Orleans. Given how few people live on the island, it can seem that the dead outnumber the living.

Corsican history is full of conquest. For centuries, up until the mid-1700s, just about every neighboring country was willing to fight for the island. It has been French for over 200 years, still there is a passionate nationalist movement seeking to reclaim Corsica's independence.

On a wall outside every village church or on a pedestal or fountain in each town square, there are long lists of engraved names of the village boys who died in one of the World Wars. There are a lot of Albertinis, Marchettis and Simonettis listed on the wall outside Tralonca's church. Those three families still live in our village, and the families still pay their respects.

Corsicans were sent by the French state to fight in disproportionate numbers and lost a painfully large percentage of its male population in the wars. People still talk about it as if the conflicts happened far more recently than they did. They blame the wars for why so much of their traditional way of life was lost.

Corsica was a strange place to be while the wars in Iraq and Afghanistan were going on. On the one hand, we were so isolated from the rest of the world, living literally on a mountain in the middle of an island. On the other hand, there was this obsession with death, both past and present. Death and war seemed to be significant parts of the collective conscience.

For the most part, though, I just felt removed from the conflicts. The daily paper, *Corse-Matin*, rarely carried stories about either effort, unless European soldiers fell. When those stories did appear, I felt strangely detached. I was disturbed by how aloof I had become. I wasn't seeing the soldiers as real people with real families grieving for them. Somehow, all of the editorials I had read over the years, all the arguments I had made or overheard about whether soldiers should be there in the first place, blocked up my emotions and left me unsympathetic.

I've never liked reading stories about war. And I don't like many war films either. I have a hard time with violence and don't have a stomach for gore. But for a long time I was obsessed with *The Things They Carried* by Tim O'Brien. It's a collection of war stories like no other I've read. The focus is so close that the reader feels the full lives of each of the young soldiers O'Brien describes. The book provides a brutal look at war, not primarily in descriptions of battles and bloodshed, but through the description of the simple things that define a soldier's everyday experience, like what he carries in his backpack.

As we learn what each soldier holds and how much each item weighs and why it's needed, we feel so viscerally all the threats he faces. We're there with him, carrying all of it, too, feeling more and more weighed down with every piece of gear named. Some of the items listed are obvious: weapons, fatigues, ammunition, dog tags, food rations, cigarettes, extra socks. Some are personal: pictures of girlfriends or siblings or parents, comic books, condoms, Bibles. Some are light: bandages, bug spray, breath mints, playing cards. Some are very heavy: a twenty-six-pound battery, a big radio, guns. And some things have no physical weight at all but are actually the hardest and heaviest things to hold: anger, hatred, distrust, longing, memories, fear.

In talking to Sarah one night about how far I felt from the wars going on, we started talking about O'Brien's book. There's this image of a poncho in one of the stories. Soldiers carry ponchos, we're told, for the rain. It's an obvious image, easy to imagine an uncomfortable, wet hike through the jungle with water dripping off a soldier's jacket. But just when the image seems contained, O'Brien deepens it. He writes that the men also would wrap bodies in those ponchos when soldiers were wounded or killed, using them to help carry the fallen to the helicopters for evacuation. Suddenly, you're pulled in way further than you were prepared for.

As I was retelling this to Sarah, I found myself feeling some walls come down. We talked about the future, imagining Jackson getting older and the state of the world he would live in. Thinking of him potentially having to go off and risk his life started to make us nauseous.

Days later I saw some pictures in the paper of fallen British soldiers arriving back on English soil. I thought about those ponchos and how much a body weighs physically and how much a life weighs emotionally to all those who knew and loved the person. Then I thought about Jackson, how little he still weighed in my arms, how much he weighed in my heart.

***

I don't write many political songs. I have a few, but even in those, I try to obscure the details enough so that the songs don't alienate. I don't want my music to make a listener defensive, closed, guarded. I want the songs to engage on a different level than a debate, or an article or essay might. So I use different details than I would use in an argument to prove my point.

I believe music has the most power to change or alter people's opinions when done subtly, through emotions not information. Songs can create one of those increasingly rare spaces that seem safe from the reach of politics, safe from the messy surface of things—the entrenched debates, the statistics, the rhetoric. In the middle of a musical movement, be it a string quartet or even a punk song, we can retreat into a world of pure emotion, excitement, longing, fulfillment, sorrow. There can be so much emotion in certain melodies and the human voice singing those melodies. Music can occupy a magical space. To exist in that space, the lyrics can't get in the way. This is definitely not to say that lyrics can't be detailed. I love details in lyrics. But as in *The Things They Carried*, I like details that transport you rather than piss you off.

"Soldier's Song" may seem like a political song. It is a song about war, for sure. And in that way, it may seem like an anti-war song and therefore part of a long tradition of anti-war songs. But it wasn't written as a protest song. It's simpler than that. It's just a human song. It seeks to get past the politics and just into the head and heart of a frightened soldier. I wrote the song with Iraq on my mind, but it really could be about any war. In a sense, it is meant to be about all of them, thus avoiding questions about whether or not any particular conflict is justified. The politics of each war may differ, but the emotions of many soldiers probably have been a great deal alike.

While we were on Corsica, I was too often blind to those emotions, and soldiers just felt like part of an argument, numbers on a page. Casualties were just

SOLDIER'S SONG

Wo oh the weight of man.
Come lift me up.
Come take my hand.
Wo oh the weight of man.

All of the lines in the sand,
And all that we carry,
And all of our cares,
Tell me how to prepare.
Tell me how to prepare.
The sooner you're chosen,
The sooner you're damned.

Wo oh the ways of man.
The dark behind
The brightest plan.
Wo oh the ways of man.

This is the strength in my hand.
This is the strength of my hand.
This is all I can hold.
I don't care that you told me,
That you think I'm wrong.
This is not your song.
This is a soldier's song.
So try to keep your head down,
Try to understand.

Wo oh the wars of man.
And why we fall
And why we stand.
Wo oh the wars of man.

These are the sounds in the sand.
These are the sounds in the sand.
This is all I can hear.
You try to block the screaming.
You cannot block the sky.
This is a soldier's cry.

This is a soldier's cry.
And no one wants to hear it.
No one wants to hear it.
But I'm afraid to die.

Wo oh the weight of man.
Please lift me up.
Please hold my hand.
Wo oh the ways of man.
Just leave me here.
Just drop my hand.
Wo oh the wars of man
Come break my heart.
Just lay me down.
Wo oh the weight of a man.
Wo oh the weight of a man.
Wo oh the weight of a man.
Wo oh the weight of a man.

The church in Tralonca.

SOME KIND OF CURE

"Winter Winds"

There is a children's book by Leo Leonni called *A Color of His Own* that Sarah and I read to Jackson so many times on Corsica that all three of us had it pretty much memorized. The story is about a chameleon upset he isn't one consistent color like fish or pigs or elephants. He tries to stay on a leaf so he can remain green. But of course, the leaf turns yellow in the autumn and then red, and the chameleon turns, too. Eventually the leaf falls from the tree, blown off by "the winter winds." The chameleon falls as well and gets cold in the dark winter night. The resolution comes when he meets another chameleon who proposes that the two stay side by side. For although there isn't any way to stop changing, they will at least be able to change together. And so they do.

Even before Jackson fully understood the words, he never liked the page where the "winter winds" blow or the "dark winter night" that followed. He would ask me to turn the page quickly. After a while, before he would allow me to read the book at all, I would have to pledge I would skip the "dark page." He still doesn't like that page, now with a far greater understanding of language, if still not the deeper symbolism and meaning of the leaf falling from the tree and the darkness in the sky.

Just before Jackson was born, a friend gave me Marilynne Robinson's *Gilead*. It is basically a long letter written by an elderly father to his young son to be read after the old man dies. Like a lot of things I read or watched or heard in the months around Jackson's birth, the book hit me hard. It got me thinking about what I value and all the things I would one day show, teach and talk to my son about.

Perhaps since reading that book, or perhaps since being flooded by that desperate sort of love that fatherhood brings, I have had this line in my head: "All the things to say, on my dying day." The lyric was addressed to Jackson, and I would try to imagine where I would go from there, what I would tell him. But I wasn't able or willing to ever get beyond that couplet, to answer the line in a way that felt emotionally and poetically sufficient. A failure in imagination, in poetry. Or maybe it was a lack of courage.

***

As our time on Corsica was winding down, we felt a bizarre swirl of emotions. There was relief and excitement. We had survived. We were going home. Jackson would get to see his grandparents again, play in playgrounds and run around on flat stretches of grass. I wouldn't have to deal with all the frustrating cultural barriers. I would be able to speak again without having to think and work so hard. But there was also regret. Our time was over. We didn't do everything we had thought we might. We hadn't changed as much as we hoped we'd change. And surprisingly, people had just started becoming really nice to us. Perhaps it was because we had announced we were leaving, we were finally treated like family by many in our village and even by some in surrounding villages. Parties were thrown in our honor. Doors were open to places we had never been invited before. At last, we began to feel like we almost belonged in our village and on Corsica. So suddenly a large part of us didn't want to leave.

We soaked up the last several weeks with new eyes. The rivers and the mountains looked all the more vivid. The smells became that much more delicious. And the sounds—the goats traversing the hillside while we had coffee in the morning, the music of the Corsican language, the click of the Boules balls against the stone walls of the village square, the children laughing, the crackle of the fires, the bells—these sounds intoxicated us and were hard to imagine giving up. The slowness, the space, the solitude gained a palpable quality, and we savored it. All of the alienation we had felt—the homesickness, the oppression of village life, the unease of living in a foreign culture, the unrest that had fueled so many of these songs—began to dissipate and feel overblown.

But then the storms came. The wind ripped up the mountainside and tore through the little alleyways of our village. It knocked out the power. There was great thunder. The rain was tremendous, and it felt like we might wash away. Everyone retreated into their homes, sealed off their windows and doors.

When the rain stopped, there was fog like we had never seen. It engulfed our village on both sides of the mountain. We were living in a cloud. We couldn't see the church bell that hung just beside our terrace. Then the rains returned. Rivers of mud rushed down the cobblestones. And, oh, the wind. The noise of the wind at night whipping through the paths and passageways was hard to bear. Our shutters, though tightly shut, still banged violently. It felt like we were being tossed in a ship. It was December, and winter had returned.

It may or may not have related to the change in the weather, but around that time Jackson started to ask us a lot about death. I knew this would happen eventually, but I didn't think it would happen so soon. He had only just turned two! Blame it on all those damn fairy tales that begin with parents dying, kids left on doorsteps or sent to live with evil relatives. Or maybe his questions would have come anyway. Maybe we're hardwired to wonder about those things from an early age.

It was difficult to know what to say, and not simply because I wanted to buffer reality and weigh what his little mind was capable of digesting, but because I didn't always know what I actually thought. His questions forced Sarah and me to consider what we really believed. Any incomplete theories didn't hold up against Jackson's relentless cross-examination.

In trying to comfort Jackson (and myself), I made up a little melody and sang about how the winter winds raging outside would settle down. It felt metaphoric immediately, as I was trying to preemptively soothe him and keep him safe from more than just the weather that thrashed against the walls and windows of our house. Yes, the winter winds would eventually settle down. But in a larger sense, they wouldn't. Hopefully they would blow me away well before they blew him away. That was only a small comfort though, as it meant that one day he'd have to calm himself down without me holding him against my chest, without me singing him to sleep. What could I possibly say to him about that?

This thought brought me back to the lyric that had haunted me since he was born, about what I would want to say to him on my deathbed. So I started writing. I wrote verse after verse after verse. I wrote maybe twenty verses and could have written more.

***

We eventually stopped reading to Jackson from the chameleon book. He has become more interested in superheroes. Dinosaurs instead of lizards. Robots. Outer space. Bright things. Loud things. Books about wrestlers. He is still so innocent and young, still so small, but less so. And that is hard to fathom, given how tiny and unformed he was when he was just starting out.

Jackson remains in a world that is pretty much safe from winter winds that really could blow him from a tree. I would never let that happen. But of course, in the end, the winter winds will be too strong for us all. They'll blow me from the tree. And one day they will be too strong for him. He'll fall from the tree, too. I can't fix this. I can't offer any kind of cure. The best I can do is to help him for as long as I can to live a full and glowing life in the face of it all, to not turn away from difficult things, to grow with strength, with a curious mind, an adventurous spirit, and a big and open heart. As hard as it may seem, all I can do is encourage him to live as brightly and beautifully as he can, to go through the world with grace.

(*Play "Winter Winds" now.*)

WINTER WINDS

All the things to say,
On my dying day.

You know the winter winds will one day settle down.
You know the talk of spring will push us off the ground.

Oh I believe in you more than you can now know.
If I could stay right here, I'd never let you go.

This is an old refrain I used to sing to you.
You had your mother's eyes. You weren't even two
When we left Fort Greene, you were still in our arms.
We tried the best we could to keep you safe from harm.

And in the end, in the end…

We crossed the Brooklyn Bridge. We crossed the ocean wide.
We sold all of our things. We kept our open eyes.
For more than a century, took more than our blood and bones,
More than just you and me to make this place our home.
If you love someone, don't be afraid to fall.
What could it mean to win if you can't lose it all?
I know the stars they fall. Sometimes the sky falls too.
Sometimes the long freight train don't stop for me or you.

And in the end, in the end,
Keep your heart, open.

Yeah this is an old refrain I sang when you lay down.
Though it may sound the same, everything's different now.
I know you'll walk away, over that mountain there.
If I could go with you, I'd follow you everywhere.
There are some things so hard, I wish they wouldn't bruise.
Everyone that you love, you will one day lose.
And one day I'll have to go. I'll travel further still.
And I will not return, no matter how strong my will.
But you know these winter winds will soon be settling.
Even the sun will shine. One day it will be spring.

Oh it's hard, I know, to carry on.
Go with grace my son.

AFTERWORD

When it was finally time to leave Corsica, we managed to find someone to buy our little Twingo. I was far better at brokering the sale than I had been at negotiating the purchase. A few of the villagers who had been the most intimidating at first actually drove us to the port of Bastia to catch the ferry to Nice, where we then boarded a plane back to Atlanta. The Corsican parting rituals are as involved as those for greetings. We had to make multiple rounds through our village before we drove off, visiting each and every house, where we were given the bisous, invited in for coffee or whiskey or both, given cookies and charcuterie that would then need to be smuggled through customs.

It was raining that last morning, as we finally managed to free ourselves from the embraces of our well wishers and run aboard the boat (after which the ship hands immediately raised the anchor and the boat set sail). Sarah and I stood out on the deck arm in arm. Jackson was up on my shoulders getting wet. We watched the island disappear in the fog. Jackson was a year older than when we arrived, out of diapers, very verbal, with the mountains and the Mediterranean in his big blue eyes. Sarah had a suitcase of full notebooks and a hard drive of pictures and interviews. I had journals of stories and a batch of new songs.

It felt like we shared a secret, a magical and mysterious secret that, no matter how many tales we told, chapters we wrote, songs we sang, would always be our secret. With the boat now gaining speed into the open sea, we felt this secret deeply and powerfully. Moreover, we shared a life, the one and only life we had. And as we came in off the wet deck and pulled hard on the heavy door, sealing off the salty wind and waves, I believe there was a glimmer in each of our eyes. We felt so lucky to be sharing that life.

(Photo by Sarah Davis.)

ACKNOWLEDGMENTS

This work would not have been possible without a lot of peoples' patience, enthusiasm, eyes, ears and support. First on the list, on all my lists, is Sarah, who brought us to Corsica, who has always helped me to see and understand the world. She was with me when all these stories were happening, when all these songs were written. She has listened to and read everything I've ever created. She is also working on a far more probing book about Corsican music, culture and efforts to hold on to their traditions. Of similar magnitude is my gratitude to my mother, who taught me to see beauty in the world and to love the words we use to express that beauty. To Will Robertson and all my amazing friends who make music with me. Thank you to Sara Michas-Martin for the careful read. To Jamie Allen for the great ideas. To Drake Bennett and Jennifer Joel for reading very early chapters. To Ben Friedland for his patient and sensitive eye. To Thomas Bell and Harlan Coban for advice. To Amanda Case and Jeff Kilgour who read, advised, supported and now promote this book and me. To the great Michael Fusco for the beautiful design and layout, and for all the great designs and layouts we've done together. Finally a great thanks is due to the people of Tralonca who ultimately made us feel so welcome and accepted us as a part of their family. Corsica remains a sacred space in our minds and hearts.